Healing for Adults Who Grew Up in Adoption or Foster Care

of related interest

Twenty-Life Transforming Choices Adoptees Need to Make
Second Edition
Sherrie Eldridge
ISBN 978 1 84905 774 5
eISBN 978 1 78450 017 7

Building Self-Esteem in Children and Teens
Who Are Adopted or Fostered
Dr. Sue Cornbluth
Foreword by Nyleen Shaw
ISBN 978 1 84905 466 9
eISBN 978 0 85700 844 2

HEALING
FOR ADULTS
who grew up in
ADOPTION OR
FOSTER CARE

Positive Strategies for
Overcoming Emotional Challenges

RENÉE WOLFS
FOREWORD BY MARLENE VAN STEENSEL
TRANSLATED BY KATE EATON

Jessica Kingsley *Publishers*
London and Philadelphia

This translation of *De Cirkel van Verbinding, omgaan met verlies bij adoptie en pleegzorg, gids voor (jong)volwassenen* is published by arrangement with Uitgeverij Aspekt, Amersfoortsestraat 27, 3769 AD Soesterberg, The Netherlands.

English language edition first published in 2015
by Jessica Kingsley Publishers
73 Collier Street
London N1 9BE, UK
and
400 Market Street, Suite 400
Philadelphia, PA 19106, USA

www.jkp.com

Library of Congress Cataloging in Publication Data
A CIP catalog record for this book is available from the Library of Congress

British Library Cataloguing in Publication Data
A CIP catalogue record for this book is available from the British Library

ISBN 978 1 84905 555 0
eISBN 978 0 85700 988 3

Printed and bound in Great Britain

Our problem is not
that as children our needs were unmet
but that as adults they are still unmourned.

David Richo

Contents

Chapter 3 The Circle of Connecting: Coping with Loss 73

Foreword

Being introduced to this book by Renée Wolfs about loss and mourning was a unique and intense experience for me. She invited me to review her book as someone with personal and professional experience. On account of my work as a trainer for foster parents and foster children, it was also possible for me to contribute stories about their experiences. As I was reading the book, gradually it started to affect me more and more. It takes you to remote places from the past that you might not visit very often any more. Sometimes you re-encounter grief there, sometimes it's where you encounter the source of your own strength.

It was like a breath of fresh air to read about the experiences of foster children and adoptees and to see how Renée subsequently places these in the light of grief and loss. Sometimes you are lost inside the stories for a moment because they are so recognisable but then, after a little while, you find yourself safely at home again. This is because Renée proves herself to be an excellent travel guide on account of her expertise in the subject and her non-judgemental way of writing. She skilfully takes the reader with her on a journey into the themes that adult adoptees and foster children deal with or have dealt with, after which she describes how to 'find the way back home', how to arrive at your authentic self.

The all too familiar diagnosis 'attachment disorder' is not mentioned in this book. Renée steers clear of this 'labelling' and in this way normalises the feelings of loss that are hidden behind this diagnosis, which is, in my view, so desperate. She places the feelings of pain and wanting in a perfectly normal, human light, thereby looking at adult foster children and adoptees who have to cope with significant experiences of loss in a very respectful way. At the same time she hands social workers and parents a wonderful tool: an emphatic, non-judgemental view with which they can guide adopted and foster children through their mourning process.

In my training practice foster children often say: *'I act tough on the outside but I'm scared on the inside.'* It seems as if a kind of 'stillness' has occurred as a result of the trauma of, among other things, having been placed in care; as if they still need to hold their breath and cannot (yet) commit to living the rest of their lives. With her model *The Circle of Connecting* Renée gives very basic and simple tools to adults, social workers and parents to help them leave this stillness behind. Her model for grieving addresses the circle of life, part of which is saying farewell. It also deals with learning once more how to breathe, inhaling and exhaling, how to internalise your personal history and to connect with its power.

Although every adoptee and former foster child has his or her own story, I am convinced that each of them will recognise him- or herself in the many stories that have been recorded in this book with such respect and empathy, and that everyone can put this book to good use in his or her own way. Let yourself be inspired and moved by this lovely and intense book.

It deals with the pain of loss but with restoring connections, too. It's about coming home, really.

MARLENE VAN STEENSEL
Founder of and trainer at Be4you2.nl and former foster child

Acknowledgements

Without the sun, the soil and the rain, nothing grows. The same holds true for this book. Without the people around me, there would not have been a harvest. First, I owe much to the Dutch and Belgian authors who went before me in writing about experiences of loss in adoption and foster care. I would therefore like to thank those authors: René Hoksbergen, Marina van Dongen, Tim de Jong, Cornelie van Well, Robin Broos and Xavier Vankeirsbulck. They all recorded intense stories about the experiences of adult adoptees and foster children. In many places these stories have firmly grounded my book.

I would also like to thank all those who responded to my appeals on Twitter and Facebook to share with me their experiences. Unfortunately it is beyond the scope of the acknowledgements to thank each of you in person. Both parents and adult adoptees and foster children have shared their stories with me, which led me to a growing understanding of the core issues involved in coping with loss in adoption and foster care. I have rephrased and anonymised many of these experiences in order to record them in my book. In this respect I would especially like to thank Marlene van Steensel, who provided me with several (anonymised) stories about the experiences of adult foster children. These have created a beautiful balance between experiences of loss in adoption and foster care in my book.

My deep appreciation also goes out to trauma therapist and health-psychologist Herman de Mönnink, founder of the Dutch Loss Studies. His inspiring way of teaching instilled in me a great love for the profession. He provided me with many fundamental insights which I needed in order to write this book.

Also I am very grateful to my enthusiastic and competent reviewers. During the writing process several versions were passed in review. Every time I thought I was done, someone would provide me with a new and critical point of view on the subject. Although I sometimes thought there would never be an end to the rounds of feedback, of course the end was eventually reached. Thank you: René Hokbergen (adoptionhoksbergen. com), Herman de Mönnink (verlieskunde.nl), Irka Lenselink (buro-inzicht.nl), Marlene van Steensel (be4you2.nl), Nelleke Polderman (basictrust.com), Diny Postema (fiom.nl), Tim de Jong (timdejongcoaching.nl) and Jurrijn Tack (geadopteerd.info). Without your specific expertise this book would not have the depth of content it now has.

Finally, my deep gratitude goes out to my husband and my three children. Their loyalty and love gave me the equilibrium I needed in order to write this book. They made room for the sun, the soil and the rain that allowed the seed to come up in the end. Thank you very much!

RENÉE WOLFS

Introduction

You have opened up a book for adults who were adopted or placed into long-term foster care as children. It is about coping with loss. At a time when psychological pain is often diagnosed and treated, it is important to trust your own feelings, too. Not every kind of pain wants a diagnosis, after all. That is one of the reasons I wrote this book.

A few years ago I specialised in the topic of 'Loss Studies'. I felt strongly connected to this subject, particularly because I had experienced a number of significant losses in my life by then. During that time I read a bookshelf full of books on loss and mourning, but found it difficult to discern the 'essence of grieving' in them. Gradually I came to realise that coping with loss is not a therapeutic process for most people; all people experience loss in life and most of them will subsequently cope with it by way of trial and error. Eventually many come to a form of 'defusing' the pain, after which it becomes possible to say farewell symbolically. Often the pain will then subside and the individual will be able to go on in their present and future. Memories of what was lost are taken along and a new connection or bond will be developed with what was lost.

If you were adopted or placed into long-term foster care, you've lost (daily) contact with your birth parents during your youth. It is very likely that you will periodically experience feelings of loss because of this. As in any mourning process, there will be times in your life when you are optimistic and look toward the future and times when you look back and are more focused on what you've lost contact with. I intentionally use the phrase 'lost contact with' here and not just the word 'lost' because I believe there is an important distinction between the two. When someone dies, when you lose your job, become ill or go through a divorce, you *lose* something once and for all and you will somehow have to say farewell. In most cases, foster children and adoptees don't actually 'lose' their parents but *they lose (daily) contact.* In most cases, saying farewell does not come up. The mourning process largely consists of *the need to find* and herein, too, lies the core of the pain: foster children hope to find loving contact again; adoptees hope to find more information or a reunion with their unknown parents. And once you find those things, the mourning process does not end. For many, the hope, the pain of looking back, the searching and finding lasts their entire life. This complicates mourning such a significant loss at a young age.

This book deals with this complicated mourning process of adoptees and foster children. Many stories about loss by adult foster children and adoptees have guided me in writing my book. I hope you will gain insight from it and that you will find recognition and acknowledgement in it.

In the first half of this book I will explain how grieving processes actually work and how mourning your adoption or (long-term) foster placement is different from other kinds of mourning. In the second half I will discuss the 'Circle of Connecting'; in this circle I have brought together seven themes that can help you to mourn your history. Most of the themes in the circle are not very complicated; they do, however, require your willingness and your dedication: your 'willingness' to have a look at the things in your life that hurt you and were hurtful to you, and your 'dedication' to work towards the things that you believe in with all your heart. So that ultimately you will be able to connect with your own life. These are the principles this book asks of you. Loss is part of life, no matter what. 'Learning to cope with loss' is the only possible answer.

CHAPTER 1

Coping with Loss

Processes of change

Everyone has to deal with change in life and therefore with loss. It starts in infancy: as soon as you are born, you leave the safe warmth of your mother's womb. As soon as you to go school or into day-care, you lose your safe and familiar environment. And this happens again when you go on to the next form, when you go to secondary school, when you venture out on your own. This will go on for the rest of your life. You become attached to something; things become familiar and you feel safe and secure in the belief that you can see where your life is taking you, that you know who loves you and what, approximately, life has in store for you. And then your situation changes. Sometimes things change overnight – for example, when your parents get a divorce, if someone dear to you suddenly dies or when your house burns down. Sometimes you can see large changes coming – for example, when someone is bedridden for a long time before he dies, or because you know that you will leave home some day.

When there are structural changes in your relationships, your home situation or your dreams for the future, you need time to realise that things will be different from this moment on, that something very fundamental has happened in your present and that it will change your outlook on the present, past and future forever. Such fundamental changes are part of life; everyone experiences them in their lives, although some people come up against them at a younger age or more often than others do.

If you were adopted or placed into foster care, you have dealt with an important loss at a young age: your birth parents were unable to care for you and you grew up, temporarily or permanently, in a care unit, an institution, in foster placement or with an adoptive family. Besides this, you have, just like everybody else, experienced new losses within your care unit, the institution, your foster family or adoptive family and during your adult life. And each time you will have had to make room for the loss in your life, sometimes for a second time, sometimes for a third, fourth or fifth time even. There is a reasonably good chance that you have not been able to sufficiently integrate these losses into your life, perhaps because you were still too young, or because the circumstances in your life have not yet allowed you to create enough room to do so.

In this chapter I will explain precisely what 'coping with loss' is and what you may experience after a loss. In doing so I will focus both on loss in more general circumstances and on loss in the context of foster care and adoption. From Chapter 2 on, I will specifically address loss in adoption and long-term foster placement.

What is loss?

When you hear the word 'loss', you may well think of mourning because someone dear has passed away. And yet there are many more circumstances that will lead you into a process of mourning. For example, when you lose the use of your legs, when you lose your job, when you cannot have children or when your relationship ends. You may mourn also when you give birth to a disabled child or when you miscarry, when you go through the menopause, or if you lose your 'sense of security' as a result of abuse or an accident or an assault, for example. In this respect, Meta (35) says:

> After the accident I simply couldn't get back into the car. I realised I was vulnerable, it could happen again anytime and maybe I would

be less fortunate then. For a long time I was afraid of driving and of riding in the car with someone else. I had always been convinced that such things happened to others, not to me. But it had happened to me. Somehow I used to think that I was safe wherever I went. That has changed since the accident. It was the day that I said farewell to the childlike notion that nothing bad would ever happen to me.

Janine (31) tells about the divorce of her parents in her childhood:

I remember my mother telling us that she was going to divorce my father. My sister was there, too. My mother cried and took us in her arms. I didn't feel a thing at that moment, somehow I couldn't believe that my parents were no longer happy together. It wasn't until later, when my father actually left home, that I slowly started to realise. Suddenly we were sitting at the table with just my mother. That was weird. And yet in the beginning it seemed as if my father was at work. In my imagination he would appear at the table eventually. It took a very long time for me to realise that my dream of a happy, complete family would never be reality again.

A simple definition of loss is:

The realisation that you have lost something that was of importance in your life, like the loss of someone dear to you, your parental home, your health, your mental capacity, your job, your ideal or your dream for the future.

There are many different kinds of loss. You may, for instance, be confronted with a 'physical loss' or a 'social loss'; the latter consists of saying farewell to close friends, colleagues or relatives. There are losses that especially have a large psychological effect – when you can't have children, for example, or when you suffer from dementia.[1] To give you an idea of the kinds of circumstances in which you may encounter loss, I will give a number of examples below.

Social losses

You mourn the loss of important elements of your environment when social losses occur. Examples of this are when you have to say farewell to your family, your parents, your friends or colleagues, your neighbourhood, your school, your native country. When you are bullied or rejected, you also experience social loss.

Physical losses

Examples of these are when you are diagnosed with arthritis or diabetes, when your leg has to be amputated, you lose the use of your arm, your face is scarred, or you lose your strength with age. Incest, abuse and rape are physical losses; you lose your physical purity or integrity. When someone dies, their physical presence disappears from your life: some people particularly miss the physical contact which is no longer there.

Psychological losses

Examples of these are when you lose someone who was a part of your identity. This also happens when you are given up, when you give up a child yourself, when you are placed in foster care or when your child is placed in foster care. Some people will experience a change of personality on account of trauma, illness or ageing; in such cases people mourn the loss of their former identity. If you were abused or raped, you also experience psychological loss: you lose your security, your purity, your innocence, your ideals about a just world.

In many cases a loss will affect more than one aspect of your personality: if you lose your health, you not only have to say farewell to your body as it was but also to your identity as it was (psychological loss) or to the friends or to the team mates with whom you used to practise your sport (social loss).

In each of these circumstances something important in your life comes to a close. This will often cause you to temporarily lose your hold on life. Somehow you have to integrate the loss in your existence. The way you cope with this largely determines how you experience what you have lost.

What is a mourning process?

A mourning process is about integrating a loss into your life story. Rather than 'to let go' in a mourning process we begin 'to connect differently'; we create a new enduring connection with what we have lost. Often when going through a new phase in life we will experience new feelings about a past loss and we will want to give meaning to it once more. It is therefore a dynamic process in which you move between letting go and connecting.

The course of a mourning process is different for every person. Much of it depends on your life-style, your mourning style and your nature. Most often people are quite capable of grieving, with support from those around them.

Besides individual differences there are also a number of similarities in each mourning process. Generally speaking, it is true that mourning is an intense process of adjustment and change. Roughly you might say that you are going through a process of:

> *becoming aware – feeling pain – saying farewell – reconstructing your life*

Hardly anyone goes through this process from A to Z; mostly these *tasks of mourning* will be jumbled up.[2] One day you will feel horribly sad or angry perhaps, the next day you will be busy with your future, your life without what you have lost. One day there will be a flood of tears and the next day you can hardly believe what happened, or you will find it difficult to accept the loss or be truly aware of it. Suzanne (53), who lost her sister when she was 30, says:

> On the day I buried my sister, I bawled my eyes out. Especially the moment when her coffin was carried out of our parents' house was very difficult for me. There she went, my little sister, leaving home forever. During the following days I often walked along the beach, and my tears just kept flowing. Despair, anger and sorrow, they were all present at once. A week after the funeral I suddenly wanted to go out with my friends. We spent an entire weekend partying. Most of them thought that was weird. How could I do

that, so soon after my sister's death? But I really needed to. The sadness weighed so heavily, I just couldn't carry it all of the time. Sometimes I just wanted to forget, pretend it hadn't happened. At that time, that helped me cope as much as crying about it.

Some people feel nothing after a loss, or they quickly go back to work to keep busy. About the time after he split up with his girlfriend, Jeremy (28) says:

> When my girlfriend broke up with me after five years, I booked a holiday with a close friend straight away. Many people thought that was strange and said that I probably hadn't cared about my girlfriend, but that was not it at all. I just couldn't deal with having to think about it all day long. We had lived together for four years and suddenly I was living alone again. I really couldn't deal with that loneliness. It helped me tremendously to take some distance and even joke about it. In this way I could gradually get used to the idea that our relationship had come to an end. Doing fun things in the meantime gave me just the amount of self-confidence I needed to get through it all.

Whether you deny the loss, become angry or allow yourself to cry, all of these feelings will simply be present in a mourning process. Generally, you pass alternatively through lighter and heavier periods. Sometimes you connect with the loss by experiencing pain. At other moments you'll be especially busy letting go and you'll then be looking to the future. You will be, then, alternatively 'loss-oriented' or 'constructive-orientated'.[3] By being 'constructive-orientated' you'll protect yourself against feeling too much pain. You'll also be helping yourself by preparing for a future without the person or thing that you've lost.

Most people prefer one kind of behaviour or the other. Some have the tendency especially to be loss-oriented, while others tend more to be constructive-orientated. Everyone has his own way. If there's no alternation at all between the two states, then it can be helpful to look at the other side, too.

During important moments of change in your life, there's a good chance that you will re-experience a loss that took place earlier in your life and that you'll want to connect with it again. Mourning can be intense due to feelings of loss, guilt, shame or anger, but it can also be filled with gratitude and beautiful memories. For Anouk (52), who lost her husband when he committed suicide, it is a life-long process:[4]

> My second husband ended his life abruptly. I was angry with him, terribly angry, especially because he had abandoned his children; at least that's how it felt at first. The children also struggled with those feelings: 'He doesn't seem to have thought that I was important enough to go on living for.'
>
> It's only now, after so many years, that I'm able to see and really feel that he was seriously ill and that the illness caused his death. I can now think about him in a loving way again. That's not to say that the anger is completely gone. Last summer, when I was carrying furniture through the rain for my son, who was moving to Delft, and I ran into all the fathers in the corridor of the dormitory, I was cursing Herman inside: 'Hey, where are you now? You should have been here.'

What themes are involved in a mourning process?

No two mourning processes are the same. There are, nevertheless, common themes. I discuss, below, nine themes that are often present.[5]

Denial and disbelief: recognising the loss

The full impact of a loss isn't always felt immediately. You'll need time to realise your life will never be the same. This may take longer for one person than for another. So a sudden loss can come over you so powerfully that it might take weeks, months or even years for you to get used to the idea that someone or something is actually not there any more.

Usually you only dare to process a loss when enough time has passed and you feel strong enough to bear the pain. And a loss can cause so much pain that it can take you your entire life to allow the pain in bit by bit.

Children mourn 'in bits' even more than adults do: one moment they're intensely busy with it, and the next it's as if nothing has happened. The realisation of what has happened will change in each new phase of a child's development.

It can be helpful to finally come to a recognition of the reality of what has happened, but only at your own pace.

Dealing with the pain, with the chaos of feelings and thoughts

When the pain of a loss hits you, you don't only feel sadness. The pain can also manifest itself as anger, shame or feelings of guilt. Other feelings that are often present are regret, fear, guilt, jealousy, relief, loneliness or feelings of abandonment. There also may be confusion, powerlessness, loss of the will to live, numbness, joy or insecurity.

How you deal with these feelings and thoughts is very personal. It depends, among other things, on your 'life-style'; are you more constructive- or loss-oriented? Are you someone who tends to think, act or feel? It also depends on the way you were raised: how have you learned, as a child, to deal with sadness or setbacks? In addition, your history will have a strong influence: if you've experienced a lot, it's often more difficult to really allow yourself to feel the pain deeply. Finally, the extent of support that you get from your surroundings will also influence how you deal with pain: if you feel safe and supported, you'll dare to express your feelings more quickly.

In order to bear the pain, many people allow themselves occasionally to be constructive-orientated – for example, by taking pleasure in brief moments of hope, pleasure and love. The more you have experienced your feelings and shared them with others, the less intense they will become.

Asking for support from those around you

Asking for support from those close to you is something that many people who are mourning find difficult. Following an acute loss, it's usually possible to find support during the first few weeks.

People empathise with you and they're there for you without having to be asked. But after the first few weeks or months it gets more difficult. The people close to you are getting back to their ordinary lives and they are not so aware of your pain. They seem to be less interested. In part, that's because many of them don't realise what you're going through: they often imagine that the sadness is over after a few weeks or months, or that you don't want to talk about it any more.

It's also more difficult to get support if you've postponed mourning or are mourning once again about something that happened longer ago. Suddenly you're sad or angry about something that you previously have rarely talked about. People often don't realise that a loss can 'suddenly' play up again, even years later.

However difficult you might find it, it is important to openly seek support now. Support from the people around you is one of the most important stress-reducing factors for people in mourning (see section 'How much support are you getting from those around you?' on p.36).

Getting on with your life: fatigue, gloom

There will come a time when people are less interested in the story of your loss. This is often a tough period in which you'll need to find a way of getting on with your daily life, with work, your family, your friends, your leisure time. There's a good chance that for a long time you'll have the feeling that you aren't functioning well. You let the housekeeping slide or neglect your health, social contacts or hobbies. Gloom and fatigue are normal in this period and it can take a long time before you begin to have more energy and to feel happier. The pain that you're still feeling takes so much of your energy that you have little left over. It is best to use the energy that you do have to do things you enjoy and be patient with yourself: it will get better, but that takes time. Eat healthy foods, don't drink too much alcohol, keep fit and be kind to yourself. If you take good care of yourself, you're more likely to enjoy a healthy recovery.

Saying farewell

Saying farewell to what you have lost is an important part of the mourning process, even if the loss happened longer ago. During a funeral, many people say farewell for the first time in a ritualised way to someone who has died. This leave-taking can be very comforting for those left behind, who will carry the memory with them for the rest of their lives. If a company closes its doors or if someone retires, farewell ceremonies are often organised, too. By means of leave-taking rituals, an important phase of life is acknowledged. You make the significance that the loss has for you symbolically visible. By acknowledging the pain of the loss, you can connect with it in a new way. You also keep the memory of the lost one alive. You take on a new, symbolic bond with it. By means of a leave-taking ritual, you give form to the process of letting go and connecting.

Keeping memories alive

Dealing with memories can be complicated. There aren't always good memories. It can also be difficult to connect with the good memories because they confront you with the time when the loss hadn't happened. The pain of the loss then becomes very tangible again. Still, it can be important to connect with these memories so that you can build a bridge between present, past and future; sometimes that's necessary for giving yourself some peace of mind and moving forward. Then you can experience not only the pain which the memories hold but also the love. In that way, someone goes with you into the future.

Sometimes you only have painful memories. To cope with these, it can help to try to discover how tainted your memories are. Maybe you or others close to you can give your memories another colour. Looking for positive memories can also help; they might be hidden deep in your mind. Bringing them to the fore again can help you to create a positive connection with the one you have lost. It's also important not to close your eyes to the negative memories that might be there. These, too, helped to make you who you are now. If you are able to accept them, you'll probably find more peace and you'll create the space to make different choices in your life.

Who am I without the one or without what I've lost?

We all have an 'autobiographical self', a self-image that is based on, among other things, your own past, present and expectations for the future. Your self-image is also based on your relationships with your family and friends, your background and much, much more. If you lose something that was an important part of your life story, you also lose a piece of yourself. If, for example, you lose your father, no one will ever look at you again with just those eyes. You aren't his daughter or 'his little girl' any more. Or if you lose your health or a dream about your future, for example, you lose a piece of your identity. People in mourning often ask themselves: 'Who am I without that other person?' Or: 'Who am I without my health, my native country, my house, my dreams for the future?' If what you've lost has given you considerable self-confidence, then it often is much more difficult to define yourself again than it would be if you also draw lots of self-confidence from within yourself and from others.

If you were placed into care or were adopted and you don't know your birth father or mother, this issue is often complicated. You cannot define yourself then on the basis of the important other. The question 'Who am I without the other?' is thus difficult to answer.

Giving meaning as the gate to a new chapter of life

After a loss, most people try to make sense of it. They do that almost automatically. If a loss is experienced as being meaningless, the future or 'fate' becomes bleak and empty. Someone who succeeds in giving meaning to a loss is more likely to adjust positively to his new situation. 'We will not waste your sacrifice' was the text under a photo of the 23-year-old student from New Delhi who died after being brutally assaulted and gang-raped on a bus. Her death sparked intense anger among the populace and mass protests on the streets. By taking to the streets against the sorry state of women's rights, people wanted to ensure that she didn't suffer for nothing.

Giving form to a new future

At the same time that you are feeling the pain of loss, you have to adapt to life without the one you have lost. It is a process of connecting and letting go, of being loss-orientated and constructive-orientated. You'll have to change your routines and activities. Your life will be different whether you like it or not. What space will you occupy now? What memories do you have of the one you've lost, and how can you give those memories a place in your life? Who are you without the one who meant so much to you? What strengths do you have? How can you take advantage of them? What is most important to you in life? How can you carry with you in life what you have lost? How did it shape you? All of these are questions that will preoccupy you when you are mourning. Keep in mind that it might take time and that you possibly will change because of what has happened.

Postponed, accumulated and complicated grief

Postponed grief

Due to a variety of circumstances you may be unable to grieve. You'll postpone your feelings until a later moment in life. We speak, then, of 'postponed grief'. The feelings that you are unable to experience at the moment of the loss, you experience at a later moment in your life.

Reasons you might postpone grief can be:

- You are naturally inclined to be constructive-orientated, which means that you don't quickly pay attention to your feelings of loss.

- You've learned from your parents/care-providers that feelings are not so important.

- Your parents/care-providers were not able to deal with their own losses in life, and therefore they were unable to teach you how to deal with feelings of loss.

- You haven't built up sufficient basic trust in your youth, so you lacked the strength to connect with the loss.

- You have experienced trauma during your childhood and were unable to (fully) process this; there wasn't any room for being loss-orientated.

- Your parents/care-providers were not or not sufficiently available emotionally.

- You hadn't felt the necessity of concerning yourself with the loss earlier in your life.

- Your focus during childhood was on other things; you were more concerned with the progress of your development or you just had to 'survive'.

- You experienced a lot of stress in your early years, which makes it difficult to regulate your emotions well (see section 'Diminished stress regulation' on p.66).

- You had responsibilities at the moment of loss, which meant that you were especially constructive-orientated.

Caren (50) lost her husband when her children were still young:

> My children were six and eight when Simon died in a car accident. In the years after, I put myself on automatic pilot. I was the breadwinner and I kept working full-time. I wanted things to be as normal as possible, to keep going for the children. It was only after five years that I ground to a halt, literally and figuratively. I ended up in the hospital with a slipped disc and multiple infections in my joints.

Many foster and adopted children are focused above all on the future and 'survival', and don't have room to grieve for the loss of their birth parents. Children who feel safe at home and who are given the room for feelings of loss by their care-providers are more likely to express their feelings and thoughts about it more often. As they begin to understand the loss more fully and as they mature emotionally, they will have other feelings and thoughts about what has happened to them. In every phase of life, new questions and feelings will surface. In such a case, the grief will not be postponed and a child will learn to deal with the loss in a more natural way. During adulthood, a person will once again reconsider the loss in every phase of life and with every life-event and give meaning to it in a new way.

Accumulated grief

If you have experienced *a number of losses* in your life and if you have been unable, again and again, to connect with the pain of these losses, that is a case of 'accumulated grief'. The losses from your past with which you have been unable to connect are an obstacle to grieving over the new loss. The pain of these losses has, you might say, accumulated. De Mönnink (2010) compares accumulated losses with a smouldering peat fire: if a peat fire is not effectively put out, it will smoulder beneath the surface. A little bit of oxygen can then be enough to rekindle the fire. If the fire is then once again inadequately extinguished, various subsurface seats of fires will smoulder, each of which can flare up with a bit of oxygen. If in your life you have been unable to sufficiently process your losses and have not been able to take leave effectively, then the losses will continue to smoulder beneath the surface. All of those unacknowledged feelings of loss are stored away as (restrained or repressed) energy in your body; they remain present in your body just like smouldering peat fires. Eventually, people often experience vague, persistent physical or psychological problems. In cases of accumulated grief, it can be helpful to look for specialised care from a professional who can chart, together with you, the history of loss. In that way, you can dismantle the pain step by step and find some peace of mind. Foster child Chiara (45) says this:

When I was 41, I experienced a burn-out. I was totally unable to cope. I couldn't understand how it had happened to me. I had always been strong and a reliable, ambitious colleague, hadn't I? I suffered from shortness of breath and eczema. My GP referred me to a grief therapist because I've had a turbulent life. At age three I was placed in care because my father didn't look after me properly. My mother died when I was one and a half. It's strange, but I only felt the pain from that with my grief therapist. I'd been carrying it with me for years without thinking much about it. I'd been getting by on 'survival mode', like before. I'd even managed to keep a very good job. It's only now that I understand how all of those painful things can accumulate in your life without you realising it, and how much of an influence that can have on you.

Complicated grief

Some people have experienced so much or have postponed grieving for so long that they have to deal with *complicated grief* in the end. It's difficult to define when that happens. De Mönnink (2010) uses the term *damage criterion* for it. According to de Mönnink, complicated grief comes into play in any case when you inflict or are in danger of inflicting damage on yourself or your surroundings; you are then a threat to yourself or your surroundings. This can express itself through neglect of oneself, self-mutilation or addiction, but also in suicidal thoughts, suicide attempts or seriously aggressive behaviour towards others.

If you experience serious problems in everyday life, it is always advisable to consult a grief specialist.

Trauma

Some losses are unexpected and shocking in a way that your senses become overwhelmed. In such cases we speak of a 'trauma' or a 'traumatic loss'. You can think, for example, of witnessing a fire, an accident, a violent crime, a natural disaster, abuse, rape and suicide; the experience of violence in war or a terrorist attack can also cause you to be traumatised. Since a traumatic experience always happens unexpectedly, you cannot prepare for it. And as a result it doesn't allow you take leave. Children can also be traumatised if they are suddenly separated from their daily care-providers. If they are still very young at the time of separation, they are often unable to remember this traumatic loss; it remains, then, stored away in their body (see section 'Unprocessed traumatic experiences' on p.69).

If you have been traumatised, then you don't immediately engage in a process of mourning. What you have experienced first summons up feelings of disbelief, bewilderment, dismay and powerlessness. After a traumatic experience, people are usually deeply upset. Most adults, however, are able to deal with a traumatic experience on their own. Support from your friends, partner and family helps in the process. Approximately 20 per cent continue to have serious, chronic problems and will need help.[6] After a traumatic experience, most people become fearful and ill; they *re-experience* what has happened both during the day and at night; at the same time, they try everything they can to avoid thinking about it (*avoidance*). In addition they also temporarily have a strong feeling of *heightened watchfulness*. Usually people have a strong need to talk about it a lot with others. By re-experiencing it and talking about it, the traumatic experience becomes more 'ordinary', so the intense feelings can slowly become more normal. It helps some people to write about it or draw. It is important not to repress the experience but to defuse it.

If the intense reactions have not lessened significantly after about three to six months and the stress is preventing you from functioning privately and socially, you should seek help. Only when the memories of the trauma have been effectively 'normalised' or 'neutralised' will there be space for a process of mourning. If you want to know more about processing trauma, you can find a number of accessible titles in the Further Reading list.

Three factors that influence the mourning process

In this section I will identify the three most important influencing factors in a process of mourning.[7] It is important that proportionate amounts of attention be devoted to each of these three factors.

How intensely do you experience the loss?

How intensely you experience a loss depends among other things on how much the loss meant to you. If your job is the most important thing in your life, then being made redundant can be much more of a blow than it is for someone who also derives much satisfaction from his or her family life, friends, partner or hobby.

Sometimes a loss has extra impact due to its sudden or traumatic character. Jay (52), for example, who lost his sister to cancer and his father to a car accident, has this to say:

> My sister and I lived toward the end very consciously. It was unbelievably sad, but in the end it was good. We were able to say goodbye to each other in a very loving way. The death of my father was much more abrupt. The period of mourning which followed was so intense; all of a sudden he wasn't there any more. I couldn't talk with him. I struggled with that for months, years in fact. I couldn't accept that he wasn't there any more.

Margy (49) lost her mother to Alzheimer's:

> My mother was still young. She was only 57 when she died. She had Alzheimer's. I always find it difficult to think back to that time. Her life was so desperate and sad. The medicine didn't have any effect. She was permanently in a state of panic. And there was nothing I could do. She was just floating there, so very lonely, in a little boat on a wild, stormy sea. In the end, she died quite quickly. I was so relieved for her that it was over. It's already five years ago now, but I still feel a great deal of pain. There's no consolation to be had from her death and that feels very heavy.

You also experience a loss more intensely if there have been accumulated losses in your life. A new loss can summon up the pain from earlier losses in a particularly intense way.

If you have been able earlier in your life to find a balance between connecting with a loss and letting it go, this might mean that you've developed greater strength for coping; in that case, your history of losses might have a positive influence on new events in your life. Your 'history of loss' can, then, have a positive as well as a negative influence.

Outsiders aren't always able to judge how much influence a loss has on someone. Sometimes what appears to be a 'small loss' has a much greater impact than what appears to be a 'major loss'. Much depends on what you've already experienced and how important something or someone has been for you. Foster child Josephine (35) says:

> My boyfriend ended our relationship. I was 25 and my world collapsed. For some reason, this event swept away the very ground under my feet. For days on end, I hid myself at home like a frightened little girl. I didn't dare to go out on the street. I had girlfriends who tried to cheer me up. They said that it really wasn't so bad; we'd only had a relationship for a year and before that I had been happy. They meant well, but it didn't help me one bit. I was alone again now, just like when my mother died when I was eight years old. He was the first boy in my life that I'd really loved. I had completely opened up to him, something that had never happened before, not even with my closest girlfriend. I thought that we were meant for each other and in my mind I had planned out my entire future with him.

How are you coping with the loss?

How you cope with a loss is in a large part determined by:

- *Your character (nature)*: some people are mostly constructive-orientated, others mostly loss-orientated.

- *Your culture, your surroundings and the way you were raised (nurture)*: this has to do with the way that you have learned to live and to cope with loss.

- *Your history*: if you've already experienced a lot or if you're in a complex life situation, that will have an influence on how you cope with a loss.

- *Your emotion-regulation*: if, at the beginning of your life, you have been mistreated, neglected or undernourished, or if your mother was an addict when she was pregnant with you, there's a good chance that you experienced feelings of stress and that these have not been sufficiently soothed by sensitive and responsive parents or carers. Your stress-regulatory system has probably not, then, been properly adjusted. As a result it is likely that you are less able to regulate/control your emotions; you might have the feeling that, as a consequence, you can get 'overwhelmed'. You might also have developed fear of emotions if you were unable, in your early youth, to create safe connections. A result can be that you don't dare to express painful emotions and that you develop a variety of vague physical complaints. I will discuss these in greater detail in Chapter 2. In Chapter 4, I will discuss how you can cope with them.

At moments of loss, people often display a strong side of their character (*nature*): in order to survive, they (unconsciously) put their optimistic character to the foreground, or they withdraw, become hyperactive, hyper-social or display their contrary, angry side. Ann's foster mother says:

> When our foster daughter came to us, she was four years old. For a very long time, she was extremely sociable. She got compliments from everyone because she was always so cheerful and attentive. She was a proper Little Miss Sunshine. We always praised her for that. But it was also very strange. She'd experienced so much. It seemed as if she just wanted to forget it. Eventually, that all changed with puberty. Her sunny disposition disappeared quite suddenly. I think that she wanted to be strong all those years. She loved the

compliments, but finally she had to make room for the other side. She'd experienced so much, after all.

Your convictions / notions about yourself also determine how you cope with losses. Maybe you learned earlier that 'boys don't cry', or 'talking doesn't solve anything' (*nurture*). You often carry ideas like these with you without being aware of them, and they can represent a major obstacle to mourning. Dick (35) says:

> In our home, no one ever discussed their feelings. I can remember that my younger sister was in a car accident. She ended up in a wheelchair and that was extremely serious. But my parents remained strong and they kept stressing that it was wonderful that she was still alive. My sister's whole world changed. She couldn't do anything for herself any more and also had to give up her hobbies. But no one talked about it. In my parents' opinion, sadness wasn't good for you. It only made things worse.
>
> I frequently catch myself thinking along those same lines. If someone is sad, I'm always inclined to smooth things over. I deal with my own sadness in the same way.

Foster and adopted daughter Els (48) had already taught herself at a very early age that she had to be strong and tough. She hardly ever talked about her problems:[8]

> I have [in my programme of study] discussed my childhood sometimes with another student, but he couldn't really do anything with it, he said. But it gave me the chance to tell my story, at least superficially. It was something I couldn't really talk about. It expressed itself in frequent migraines. My feelings were locked up inside. Other people always brought their problems to me, trusted me with them. But I rarely talked about my problems with others. I was strong and tough.

How much support are you getting from those around you?

Support from those around you is one of the most important stress-reducing factors in mourning. The important thing about social support is that someone is an 'anchor' for you or a 'a sturdy tree' that you can lean against; a friend or a teacher can have that role, for example, as well as parents or family. Jerry (41) says:

> After my wife died, I got the most support from my brother. We didn't even talk all that much, but we just had a weekly meeting. He would come for a visit every Saturday. He cooked for our family, he did something fun with the children and in the evening we watched a good detective. It was really good. It was a comfort to me that he was always there. I wasn't alone.

Although many people find it difficult to ask for support in situations of loss, it's very important that you do. Those around you can't tell what you need. It's best if you let them know yourself. Think about who you can ask for help. Is there someone you can agree to play a sport with or eat with regularly? Someone who can run an errand for you? Someone you can go for a walk with on the beach? Are there people with a similar experience with whom you can share your story? And ask yourself whether you are ready to *receive* support. Your trust in others and your attachment patterns are important in this regard.

Questions
Knowledge questions

1. Why can't you subdivide a process of mourning into phases or steps?

2. What is postponed grief? What is its function?

3. When can one speak of accumulated grief? What can happen in cases of a new loss?

4. Why is it that you can't compare one loss with another? That you can't say that one loss is heavier than another?

5. Why is it not always the case that you have to 're-experience the intense pain of a loss'?

Personal questions

1. In a process of mourning, people alternate between letting go and connecting. What do you think of when you think of letting go? What does connecting mean to you?

2. What is the use of alternating between being loss-orientated and constructive-orientated? Which was your preference as a child? Do you know why?

3. Which themes play a role in a process of mourning? Name four. Which themes fit your life-style best?

4. Your history of loss but also your character (nature), the way that you were raised and your life-style (nurture) determine to a large extent how you cope with losses. The extent to which you are able to regulate your emotions also plays an important role. What is that like for you? What are the most characteristic/determining elements for you?

5. How do you mourn? Where do you place yourself in the process between letting go and connecting? Do you have a preference for one or the other, or not at all? Why is that?

CHAPTER 2

Mourning the Core Loss

Themes of loss in long-term foster placement and adoption

If you have been adopted or placed in foster care, then during your youth you have lost contact with your birth parents in your daily life. It's very likely that sometimes in your life you will experience feelings of loss. Just as with every process of mourning, you will at times be loss-orientated or constructive-orientated: during some periods you'll be looking backwards and will be focused on what you have lost contact with, and during other periods you'll be looking forward and will be more optimistic. I'm deliberately using the phrase *'what you have lost contact with'* and not just the phrase *'what you have lost'* because there's an important distinction involved. If you *lose* someone or something, you can create the opportunity to say farewell, which gives you a chance to re-establish a new and different connection with what you have lost. Foster and adoption children don't usually lose their parents, but *they lose contact with them*. That means that there's no question of saying farewell; even if the birth parents are completely out of the picture, the hope remains of re-establishing contact in the future. As a result, the process of mourning has to do to a large extent with *the need to find* and that is often where the nucleus of the pain can be found: foster children hope that they will re-discover a loving relationship with their parents; adoptees often long to find out more about the reason for their relinquishment or for a reunion with their unknown parents. For many, the hope, the pain and the restless search last their whole life. During their lives adoptees and foster children may mourn:

- the rejection or abandonment by the biological parents

- the absence of a 'normal', reciprocal relationship with the birth parents; many continue to long for such a connection for their whole lives

- the lack of the biological parents

- the painful things that happened at home in their youth; the pain can manifest itself as sadness, but also as anger, fear, disbelief/confusion, guilt or shame

- the absence of 'primal recognition' (if they (still) don't know their parents)

- the lack of the original language and/or culture

- the absence of important parts of the story of their life; this often results in a longing to complete the puzzle

- the distance and the language or culture barrier which stands between them and the biological family (feeling 'between two worlds' or 'between two families')

- the loss of their original name (if they are adopted).

Something that can make the process of mourning for the core loss even more complicated is the fact that adoptees and foster children are also confronted with new losses during their lives. If you have to move house, or if you're involved in a divorce, or are bullied at school, or are involved in someone losing his or her job, or in someone's serious illness, or the divorce or death of someone close to you, the pain of the core loss can come right back, and it can be difficult to understand exactly what you are mourning. Sabine Noten (2009) describes this as 'accumulated sadness' and uses the metaphor of a set of rocks piled on top of one another: the rock on the bottom represents the core loss, and on top of it come the new, significant losses. The rock on the bottom represents the foundation; if this 'core loss' is insufficiently 'seen' or 'acknowledged', the pile of rocks will never be stable.

In this chapter, I will address those specific things that adoptees and foster children will mourn as children, adolescents and adults. Since it can be revealing to look back to your feelings of grief in childhood, I will discuss these in considerable detail. At the end of the chapter, I will consider a number of factors that may hinder your process of grieving. I expect that they will give you more insight into the core loss and into your own process of mourning.

Children

For growing children, grieving about being given up for adoption or placed in foster care is complicated. As a result of the fact that they are maturing intellectually and emotionally, every few years they will look differently at what has happened. What's more, it's often difficult for children to say exactly what they're feeling or thinking. Often they unconsciously reveal their pain through their behaviour: they become quiet/withdrawn or they become very active or angry instead. Other children conform, out of fear, and behave in socially desirable ways. And, again, other children lapse into 'regression'; they behave, temporarily, in a somewhat less mature way than their peers.

Denial as a method of self-protection

It often takes a long time before adoptees and foster children are able to allow the pain that they feel about the core loss to express itself. There's a very good chance that they are still not able to experience the tangle of emotions because they do not feel safe enough, or because they still lack the necessary strength. Long after the adoption or placement in foster care they might still have the feeling that there's nothing the matter. To the outside world, these children look unaffected; they just get on with their daily activities and are confident that things will get back to normal again.

At primary school age, they often make use of this denial mechanism unconsciously. They might very well tell others that they have no problem at all being adopted or placed into a foster home. They might keep a very diplomatic distance and deflect any attempt their adoptive or foster parents might make to discuss their past. Consider, for example, the case of adoptee Sam (11):

> Our son is very sensitive. He can be intensely sad because he doesn't know his first mother. I always try to be there for him then. There are periods when he doesn't want to talk about the country where he was born or about his mother at all. Those are the moments when it's all too much for him. Especially at school he doesn't want to talk about it; he's afraid he'll break down in tears. We talk about it sometimes at home, but certainly not too much. I try to respond to the feelings that he expresses; I think it's just all too much for him and that he can only face it in small pieces.

Some children have extremely positive fantasies about their birth parents for a long time. There's a very good chance that they do that because the unpleasant things that they've experienced have too much impact on them.

It is important to realise that denial in children can be very functional; as long as it doesn't become too extreme, it often works as a safety device. A child can only manage without his denial mechanism when he feels safe and emotionally strong enough to face the situation and experience the pain of loss. Some children are only emotionally strong enough when they have reached adulthood.

Denial can also be motivated by loyalty, because you are dependent on your carers or because you are mainly trying to survive. Former foster child Marilyn (53) tells about her youth:

> I often isolated myself because I didn't know exactly what was expected of me and how people would react to my answers. Sometimes you express yourself positively because you calculate that you increase your chances of survival that way. Anyway, when I was ten I had no idea whether I was speaking 'positively' or 'negatively' about my father. That was a qualification adults gave to

what I said. The situation was what it was, and I had to deal with it. Sadness was far beyond my most distant horizon.

Acute mourning after placement
BABIES AND TODDLERS

After placement with their new family, babies and toddlers miss above all the familiar rhythm, the familiar sounds and smells, their carers who gave them food and kept them clean. These children show that they're unhappy especially with body language. If very small children feel safe and if the primary carers recognise and acknowledge their sadness, then they will feel able to express their sadness/lack in an appropriate way. If it is not recognised and acknowledged or if the baby or toddler does not feel safe, then he will generally not express his sadness. The memory of the loss will then be 'remembered' in the body and later in life it will probably try to find a means of expression by way of physical complaints, behavioural problems or learning difficulties.

New pain about the loss often comes to the surface again ('piece by piece') in a new developmental phase or as the child suffers new losses. Ideally the new carers are able to allow the young child to feel the pain. The warmth in a voice and giving a name to the pain can help to make a young child feel safe and comforted. The pain that the child feels can be soothed too with lots of physical contact, provided the child responds well to this. In this way, feelings of loss can be put to rest to some degree. Adoptive mother Eva says:

> We went to China for our daughter when she was 12 months old. She was obviously used to lots of people and was always laughing at everybody. The laughter lasted a few months. We provided her with safety and structure the whole time. It was only after six months that she became sad. She started to cry at night. We used to pick her up then and comfort her. I would put her in my lap or carry her and we would talk about China. I knew that she couldn't literally understand what I said, but it seemed as if I should give what had happened to her a name. Carrying her and talking calmed her down. Usually she was quiet again after half an hour or so.

Children who have experienced one or more traumatic losses before being placed with a new family often need professional supervision. If they can't neutralise their anxious memories, the fear will not end. Barbara (37), who was traumatised by war, has this to say about the period after her adoption from Beirut[9]:

> I came from far away. For as long as I can remember I've been extremely scared. Scared of the dark, scared of being alone. From the time when I was three years old, I've been sick to my stomach in bed four nights a week out of fear. [...] I can still remember exactly how I felt: blind panic. Scared of sirens, ambulances, air raid alarms, fire, death. It was of course war trauma, but the GP didn't realise it. He said: 'She's a troublesome child. Just let her cry! And otherwise give her a slap on her bottom.' But my mother doubted that: 'Well, troublesome...I think she's just scared.' But she didn't know what to do about it either. She would come to my room and say: 'Barbara, what more can I do? I've left your nightlight on and I've read 15 stories to you. This has to stop sometime, doesn't it?' But it didn't stop. She had to stay seated at the foot of my bed, because as soon as she left the room, the fear returned. She couldn't go anywhere, because if she did, I panicked.

It is usually necessary to defuse a trauma so that the memories associated with it can to some extent be neutralised; only after that is there room for feelings of loss. If you want to know more about how children process traumatic experiences, you might find it useful to read the book *Trauma Through A Child's Eyes* by Peter Levine (see Further reading list).

PRIMARY SCHOOL AGE

Children who are already somewhat older at the time of their placement especially miss their familiar environment at first. The home, the carers, the birth parents, their old friends suddenly aren't there any more. The child has to sleep in another bed, gets different food to eat, has different carers and a new school. Adopted children often lose their mother language and have to get used to a new climate to boot. They probably often think back to the time when they were still with their birth family or in an institution, because, however difficult it might have been there, they may still experience a deep sense of loss. Because so many things have changed at the same time, it is very likely that they can't process it all at once. They probably have negative thoughts sometimes: 'If I am really good now, then I'll be allowed to go back,' or even: 'If I behave really badly, then I'll be able to go back.' They might even create a fantasy again and again that although they are here now, someone will soon come to take them back.

It's important that older children have the chance, when placed in a new home, to adjust to the new situation gradually and to share their memories. If they are sensitively received in the new situation, then they can gain comfort and support from the new contact. If the new parents/carers find it difficult to talk about the first period of the child's life – for example, because the child has experienced unpleasant things – then it is very likely that the child will (unconsciously) make the sensible decision to get on with his life and not to look back. In that case, the sadness won't get the space it needs and the child will not get the chance to carry with him the good or neutral memories that he has.

Sometimes, children have gone through so much that they cannot yet connect with their past. In that case it is important that a child feels secure and peaceful. When the child is more accustomed to the new situation, the best thing to do is ask a specialist for advice.

Existential insecurity in foster children

Where children are subject to involuntary placement, it's often not clear what will happen to them in the long term. They are usually first placed in a temporary institution or a family home. Customarily, after a period of time they're moved again. The insecurity is quite considerable in that first phase. The placement is often 'secret' and the fact alone that the parents are not allowed to know where the children are produces considerable stress, especially for the children. And they find themselves in a completely new family situation and they usually also have to go to a new school. During this period, the children often have no idea what will happen to them in the future. Is this a temporary school? Will they soon return to their own parents, to other family members or go to another foster family? What will their situation be like three or six months in the future? Sometimes a child is told informally that he will probably return to his own parents, while in fact that's not at all certain. There's also often uncertainty about the cooperation among the various organisations. Foster fathers Aad and Ron say:[10]

> Our foster son Michael was often afraid that he would have to leave. If the social worker came to our house to see how things were going with him, he'd go upstairs to pack his bag. He took it for granted that she had come to get him. He had been moved so many times in his life that he couldn't believe that he would be allowed to stay with us. So we decided to apply for custody in the hope that that might convince him that he wouldn't be taken away again. His parents agreed and then we were able to put his mind at rest.

Children in placement sometimes long deeply for their birth parents because they miss the routines and the familiarity and because they feel a basic existential loyalty to their birth parents. Sometimes this existential loyalty plays up repeatedly because a child is being put down and rejected elsewhere, too. Former foster child Anna (41) says:

> My mother was completely unable to care for me, just as her mother had been unable to care for her. She 'lent me' to various boyfriends of hers in the hope that that would convince them to stay with her. So I 'slept' between them.

> When social care placed me in foster care, I ended up in a girls' institution. From there, I was placed three times in various foster homes to see if I fitted in their families. 'On spec', you might say. I was never placed. I have never experienced anything more humiliating than that. Strangely enough, it was then that I missed my mother very much.

Sometimes foster children miss, more than anything else, the other family members or the dog, their friends or a confidant at their old school. Foster child Mischa (23) says:

> I was 12, things were extremely intense at home and so for that reason I was placed in a foster home. I was horribly mistreated by my mother as well as my father, and in principle it was good to be in a safe place finally. I didn't have to be scared any more and constantly watch my step. It was a revelation that there were also parents who were kind and loving to their children. But in the beginning I still felt horrible. Because, however bad it had been at home, I still missed my own room, my dog Tes, my friends at school. I was very homesick. Fortunately I had a very good social worker who understood my homesickness. He had the notion to ask if the dog could stay with me. Two weeks later, Tes was with me again; I cannot describe how happy I was then. I cried for joy. From then on I could always share my sadness with Tes.

As long as foster children have no certainty about their future home, they'll mainly be constructive-orientated. Only when they feel no basic existential insecurity and have had the chance to feel safe with their possible new, steady carers can they begin to allow themselves to be loss-orientated and to start connecting with the pain. This constructive-orientated behaviour can last for months, years or even an entire life, especially if children remain uncertain about where they will be living in the future.

Episodic grief during primary school age

After a period of time, adopted and foster children get used to the new customs and their new surroundings. In the most favourable circumstances, they have been able to bond with their new carer(s) and to deal with their feelings of loss. Usually this is the beginning of a quieter time.

Starting in about the seventh year, many children experience new feelings of loss; from about this age, the realisation of loss hits more deeply. Children begin to understand more clearly what has happened to them and why their parents have abandoned them.

They often start missing their biological parents or family again and find it difficult to process reality. Foster child Anna (34) says:

> I had been living with my foster parents for as long as I could remember; my mother had already passed away when I was 18 months old. There was a standard story that my parents told if anyone came to visit: 'This is Anna, our foster daughter, and she's living with us because her mother passed away and she had no family who could care for her.' This was just the story and I never gave it much thought. But at age seven all of a sudden it changed. I remember very clearly that I was lying in bed one evening and suddenly I saw my mother's face in front of me. She looked just like me and she was smiling at me. I became enormously sad. I ran downstairs and fell crying into the arms of my foster mother. I suddenly missed my mother so desperately, beyond what words can describe. Luckily I was able to share it with my foster mother really well; she thought it was very normal for me to feel this way.

Some children of primary school age fantasise frequently about 'what could have/should have been'. Or they suddenly think about the fact that they might have grandfathers, grandmothers, brothers and sister whom they don't know (well).

Since children are often unable to express the fact that they are grieving, they usually show it through their behaviour: they are more quickly angry, difficult, disappointed, quiet, sad, or they develop physical complaints. They might be troubled with feelings of shame or feel powerless about what has happened to them more than anything else. They frequently wonder, for example, why this has happened to them. They might lose their appetite or sleep badly. The child might not grow as quickly as expected, or be apathetic sometimes, or fall ill often. Some children fall, for a period of time, back into behaviour that is appropriate for a younger age. That might mean that they don't get on as well with other children in their class. They might envy their friends or other family members because they feel different or inferior. Sadness about the core loss often becomes stronger during birthdays. Foster daughter Els (46) says:[11]

My birthday was always a disaster. On the one hand, I had that somewhat happy feeling about having a birthday which a child ought to have, but I also always had that sad feeling. The feeling that I don't belong here, and where is my father, where are my brothers? I was always sad on a day like that and glad when it was over.

If children are difficult during this period, there's a good chance that their carers and teachers will confront them with their difficult behaviour and not with their underlying pain. Emmy, foster and adopted child, says:[12]

During my [birth] mother's visits I was a very well-behaved girl, because deep in my heart I hoped that they would take care of me again one day. I thought that you had to be a bad child, otherwise your mother wouldn't send you away, would she? It can't be that you're a good child if your mother sends you away. As soon as I was home [with my adoptive family], I became very angry and swore at my adoptive mother. I was a horrible child then. And then I'd go and stand in front of my adoptive mother and ask: 'Do you love me?' 'Of course,' she'd say. I said then that I hated her and ran to my room. [...] I was going to pester until she'd get tired of me too.

At these times it is important that children are allowed to express their feelings and that the parents do not pass judgement on the behaviour and the feelings that are present. In that way the child will develop the feeling that his pain is acknowledged and that he is allowed to feel the way he does.

At primary school age, some children can already recognise and express their feelings well – for example, because the carers/parents have frequently been talking about the past with the child. As a rule, children are then better able to recognise their grief and identify it for what it is. Asha (35), adopted from India, says:[13]

As a child, I often felt an emptiness inside and asked myself why nobody knew if I still had a birth family in India. I often asked my parents the same question: 'Are you sure that no one knows anything about my family in India?'

Unfortunately they couldn't help me, because they didn't know anything about my background either. The only thing that they could do was help me to learn more about Indian culture by reading books and watching films. [...] In this way I learned about parts of the country of my birth and tried to imagine what my life would have been like if I had grown up in India.

Many children with a different ethnic origin become aware during their primary school years that they are different. Leonora (39), adopted from Indonesia, says:

Once I had reached the age of nine or ten, I began to be more bothered by my adoption. Children began to comment on the colour of my skin more often. And the girls in my class were suddenly much taller than I was. I suddenly became the small, Indonesian girl. I started to feel that I was different, while before that time I hadn't.

Foster children often grieve about the lack of a self-evident relationship with their biological parents, or because they weren't well treated at home. They often keep hoping that the relationship will be re-established. They also often grieve because they're separated from their sisters, brothers and grandparents, because they miss their dog, their friends or a confidant from their old school.

Adolescents (12–24 years old)

In puberty (the early and middle adolescence, from ±12–16 years old), adoptees and foster children are involved in a process of becoming self-sufficient/autonomous. They start to untie themselves from their parents/carers and bond with them in a new, more mature way. At the same time, their bodies and brains are developing rapidly and they are undergoing huge hormonal changes and shifts, as a result of which they often look at their own lives through swiftly changing lenses. They develop their social and psychological identity, think about examinations and career choices and about the time when they will leave home. All things considered, this is a very intense period, during which it is especially complicated to pay attention to their own history of loss. Starting at about age 16 (late adolescence), more room opens up to think about their core loss.

Denial as a method of self-protection

During puberty, few foster and adopted children find the space to address the grief about the core loss. Just as with young children, this can be an unconscious way to protect themselves. It may be, for example, that they have experienced too much and first need to reach adulthood. Often the effects of the loss can only be experienced then. Sometimes denial is the result of loyalty or of feelings of dependence on the carers. Young people can also repress their feelings because they don't feel safe enough. Foster child Marilyn (53) says that she didn't want to speak about the past because she didn't want to be confronted with difficult questions:

> I have never felt ashamed that I had a different home and life-style. But I did find it difficult that it was that way. In my puberty or adolescence, you couldn't often talk about the reality of your history; if I told someone that I had been raised by several different people, I always got questioned about my emotions and my losses and I couldn't or wouldn't go into that. It was all too intense. At moments like that, I was also often confronted with value judgements, which I found very painful. Back then I was often inclined not to tell the whole story, but that meant that I was less truthful and it also wore me out.

The denial mechanism usually works unconsciously. Only later in your life can you look back and identify it. Often you need the distance of a number of years. Jan Willem (45), adopted from Greece, says:[14]

> There's a huge difference between how I experienced my youth and how I look back on it now. In hindsight, I realise that I blocked lots of emotions in order to be able to function, but I never

> realised that when I was a child. It was just a given: my brother and I were the children of our parents and we happened to come from Greece; that was it.

Sometimes there isn't enough room to talk about your loss in the family where you grow up. That, too, can mean that feelings of loss are postponed.

Episodic grief during adolescence

Some adoptees and foster children grieve in this period (once again) about the fact that they are not part of a 'genetically determined family system'. Consider the words of Ben (31), adopted from Columbia:

> What I remember more than anything else from my puberty is a feeling of loneliness, even though I wasn't alone. I had lots of friends and good adoptive parents. But my friends lived in 'ordinary' families, they looked like their father or mother and had talents that one of them had. I didn't. I didn't look anything like my adoptive parents. Not that they were annoying, not at all. They were extremely kind to me and I could be just who I was. But sometimes I still felt very lonely. I didn't know what family I came from. It was the idea that I was the beginning of a family tree and not a branch someplace in it that made me lonely. That's the feeling that I had then, and still have sometimes.

Sometimes foster children long for their home, without realising the consequences of that longing. The longing for 'normal' contact can be so powerful that they decide to return to their parent(s), even though they know it isn't good for them. Former foster child Felicité (52) says:[15]

> [When I turned 15] my mother and I spent an afternoon and an evening together. When I left, she said that I'd always be welcome with her. She meant going to live with her and her family. At the time, I didn't realise that the meeting had been a bad idea. I had all sorts of 'illusions' about having a mother of my own and 'having' my own little brother and sister. No one could keep me from going

after my illusions. When you're 15, it's difficult to face reality. Not even my foster parents could change my mind about my plans.

Internationally adopted children can experience increasingly strong feelings for their original culture and language in their puberty and adolescence. From the time that he was 18, after his first exposure to the land of his birth, Anand (36), adopted from India, turned against 'the white race' for a long time:[16]

> For a while then I was very much against the white race. Almost racist. I would rant against the apparent superiority of the white race. I once ruined the Christmas celebration at home first by starting a heated discussion about the whites who were responsible for all sorts of evils and then by leaving home in anger.

Foster children are sometimes only placed in long-term foster care during their puberty. They then feel the pain of rejection more than anything else. Former foster child Joanne (25) says:

> When I was 13, I was temporarily placed in an institution. I thought that I'd go back to my home when my mother's problems were sorted out, but after two months I was told that I would not be allowed to live at home again. My mother didn't want me to. My throat squeezed shut, I could hardly breathe. How could my mother do that to me? All of a sudden I felt completely alone in the world. I didn't belong anywhere.

If foster children and adoptees are repeatedly placed in a new family or institution, then they will experience the pain of being placed in care or of being given up even more strongly. The child is doubly rejected and the pain that it causes can lodge itself deep inside.

Adoptees and foster children sometimes grieve because they have been placed with carers where they don't feel at home, or where they might even be mistreated or abused. Foster child Emily (32) says:

> My foster father abused me. At night, he often came to me. It was horrible and I couldn't sleep a night through any more. I was always listening to hear if he was coming. If I didn't want him, he said I was

a whore and threatened to send me back to the institution. I knew it was wrong, but I kept my mouth shut. Because I didn't want to go back to the institution, and my foster mother was always very kind to me.

Some boys and girls express their anger more than anything else. They often project their pain about being given up or placed in care onto the adoptive or foster mother, as former foster child Hannah (28) says:

When I was in my puberty, I was almost impossible to control. I made a complete mess of everything. At school, I couldn't make friends; I broke things off before it got serious. And I had huge rows with my foster mother. We had fierce confrontations. Sometimes I hated her for her prudish ideas. I couldn't bear it when she was kind to me; that was like a red rag to a bull.

In retrospect, I don't think that I was really angry with her in particular, except for the usual [teenage] fights. Deep inside there was a rage simmering about what had been done to me. I hated the organisations that had taken me away from my mother. Probably I was mostly angry with my mother. But she wasn't alive any more, so my foster mother took the blame. I also think that I didn't dare to feel that pain when I was in my puberty. It was safer to shout at my foster mother. Horrible, really. The only people who are really on your side get all the shit. Fortunately, my foster parents understood that very well even then, and they were able to put my anger in the proper context. Now we have a really strong relationship.

When the turbulent developments that occur during puberty have begun to pass, a stronger feeling of emptiness or loss begins to grow, because there are parts of their life story that foster children and adoptees don't know. The longing to complete the puzzle makes many young adults take concrete action in this period. When the life story has become more complete, they can often find more peace in their present lives and look to the future. The search keeps some young adults busy for years; whatever it takes, they want to get to the bottom of it. For other young adults, to be 'busy with it now and then' suffices; they only want to collect the most important information, without undertaking a 'roots' journey or meeting people. Carers or adoptive or foster parents can (if the child indicates an interest) begin this search, together with their child; they can look for as much information as they can find together, without actually undertaking a roots-journey.

Finally, the impending moment of 'leaving home' can raise the theme of loss in adoptees and foster children in a way that demands significant attention. At that moment, they lose their parental home and/or carers and face the future on their own. Foster children and foster parents even lose governmental support when the child turns 18.

Questions such as, 'What will happen when I leave home?' and 'Who can I depend on then?' can be unsettling for adopted and foster children and can confront them directly with the moment that they were left, willingly or unwillingly, by their parents.

Adults

During adulthood, most people develop the existential awareness that there are life questions that need to be answered. We are aware, for example, that we are ultimately on our own in life, a realisation that can result in feelings of loneliness and isolation. We also gradually realise that we are mortal and that life has no fixed goal or meaning. These are the big 'Why-questions' which come into focus, and we usually focus on these questions with greater intensity when important changes take place in our lives. At such times we begin to try to make sense once again of what has happened to us earlier in life.

Adult foster children and adoptees experience new feelings of grief about their adoption or placement in foster care during such periods. Many of them long once again to give meaning to what happened to them when they were young. The process of letting go and making connections can be compared to a perpetual motion machine: it is a process that goes on and on and is continually in motion.

Denial as a method of self-protection

Just like children, adults can also keep the pain of their loss at arm's length for all sorts of reasons, and that can be very functional. If, for example, you have a job that involves lots of responsibility or you have a family with children, it can be the case that, after a loss, you are mostly constructive-orientated and for a while you would rather look to the future than the past. Adoptee Melany (24) says:

> In my puberty, I was very preoccupied with my adoption. I planned to look for my mother; she's living in the same country as I do. But that plan fell through; when I was 18, I found out I was pregnant and from that moment on I had other things to worry about. When my son was born, he was found to have a heart disorder. And for that reason, he needs a lot of extra care. He's six now, and I'm always very busy with his health. Sometimes I think: Does he look like my mother? But I put that question on the back burner again; for now, my son's health is the most important issue. Maybe I'll look for her someday. But it's not as important to me as it used to be. Maybe that's because I'm a mother too now. I'm much busier with my child and not so much with myself.

If a loss has had a very large impact, it's possible that you cannot yet bear to let the pain in. Denial then works like a safe buffer against the intense feelings. Marilyn (53) says this about the anger that she felt for years, which was to her a shield against pain:

> For a long time, I covered my feelings of grief with anger. Anger is a huge motivator; it keeps you away from mourning. For a certain period of my life, that might have been a good thing. A motivator too. I did not want my father to have such an influence on me that it would destroy me and that he would have been right when he said things like: 'You're not worth anything.' I had to struggle with more than one person to prove them wrong. Social workers can also pass really ugly judgements on children, undermining their confidence. By all that fighting, I've gotten to be where I am now.

In the longer term, a denial mechanism can also work against you. You may appear 'strong' to the outside world, but it's almost impossible to make any kind of contact with your own heart or with the pain that's concealed under the protective layer.

Episodic grief in adulthood

The process of 'connecting with the pain' is often re-activated when you experience new losses, or when you enter a new phase of life. The pain can also act up on days of special significance. Cris (28), adopted from Brazil, says:[17]

> Every year on my birthday, on the night of 7 December, that same feeling of sadness comes back. I always think about my Brazilian mother then. That could also be the moment when she thinks about me. Is she well? What might she be thinking right now? Is she thinking about me? I do hope so. I usually lie awake that night and feel very sad. I don't know if she's still alive.
>
> I have that feeling of sadness more often, every few months. The feeling that you've been let down, that you're all alone, that you're on your own in the world. But I think that other people probably feel that way too sometimes.

Sometimes it's difficult for adult foster children and adoptees to know exactly what they're mourning when they experience a new loss. Every time something intense happens, the earlier feelings of loss are triggered. If you haven't had sufficient opportunity to grieve about your history, then you've not acquired the proper 'tools' for dealing with feelings of loss. That often means that it's difficult to make room for new losses. Even if you've had the chance to mourn your core loss during your childhood, it can still be difficult to distinguish between the various feelings of loss. The loss of a job or the end of a relationship can bring you right back to your very first feeling of rejection. It can be difficult to distinguish whether you're so upset in response to the job loss or if it's so intense because you were once rejected. Because of the core loss of their first parents, adoptees and foster children are usually more sensitive to rejection in any case, even when it is relatively 'small'. The rejection by the first parents is the trigger that brings this feeling to the surface: you might experience it as a rejection of your whole self.

Some adults mourn the part that is missing from their life story in particular. That sense of something missing can also begin to emerge only gradually during their lives. Adult adoptee Stephan (52) says:[18]

> If you'd talked to me about adoption 30 years ago, I would have said: that doesn't mean anything at all. I wouldn't say that any more, because in fact it means quite a lot. Because you always have the idea that you've been thrown into the middle of a story. That you don't know the beginning. There's something unpleasant about that and it remains unpleasant.

Adoptees can also feel lonely because they don't belong to a genetically related 'family-system'. Surya (40), adopted from Indonesia, says:

> I have a good life and I'm very pleased with everything I've achieved. I have a family and three beautiful children who give me great pleasure every day. It's wonderful to have a 'real' family, to see that they have my genes and those of my wife. But at the same time it still hurts that I don't know my birth family. In some way or another, that gives you a feeling of loneliness. I'm not part of a family-system, I'm at the start of one. Don't misunderstand me. I get great pleasure from the branches that have appeared after me, but I still miss my own family tree. It seems to me that that feeling of loss gets stronger as I grow older.

Sometimes adults feel as if they are standing 'between two worlds' – for example, if they have contact with their birth family. Since they've grown up in a different culture and with a different language, it's difficult to have real contact with their family, however hard they try (see Chapter 4).

As adults are able to understand the context of their adoption or care proceedings, there often is more room for acceptance, which can give them more peace of mind about their past. Looking for that context is, for many adults, a way of dealing constructively with the pain. Foster child Jenny (38) says:

Little by little over the years, I have been able to understand my father. He suffered a lot in the war and saw horrible things. He couldn't deal with that. It caused him enormous stress. As a child, I was scared of him and I still think that he shouldn't have beaten us. But now that I'm an adult, I can understand it better.

Marina van Dongen (43), adopted from Greece, developed, as she matured, a greater capacity to put things in perspective. In an interview, she says:[19]

Growing older helps you to put things in perspective. I always idealised the blood relationship between children and their birth parents. My expectations were raised very high when I became a mother myself: now I'm beginning the Marina-dynasty, I thought then, and now I know that every child is a new, completely autonomous person. Kinship with relatives cannot be taken for granted.

Life losses

Adopted and foster children experience new losses during their lives, just as everyone else does. Sometimes those losses are connected to your progression through your life cycle. One can then speak of 'transitional losses'; they take place while you are growing from one phase of life to another – for example, when you're leaving home, getting married, having a child, entering into menopause or retire. They are part of the cycle of birth, growth, death and new life. In such phases, your life can often change drastically.

Another kind of loss that everyone experiences is the so-called 'incidental loss'; incidental losses are losses that are not predictable. You lose your job, become ill, lose your partner or your child, suffer a miscarriage, become infertile, or have a disabled child. Adoption and being placed in foster care also fall into this category. Incidental losses can change the existing structure of your life dramatically. Most people try to make sense of and give meaning to these incidental losses during new phases of life.

Former foster children and adoptees are often more sensitive to new losses, especially if these losses are clearly associated with their feelings of loss about being adopted or placed in foster care. I describe, below, a number of typical situations of loss which are associated with adoption or being placed in care.

Leaving home

For many adoptees and foster children, leaving home is one of the most daunting moments of their lives since being adopted or placed in care. Emotions that have to do with the loss of their original family can come forcefully to the surface. You might be frightened that from now on you're alone in the world, just like before. Boris (28), foster child, says:

> When I turned 20, I started to live on my own. I'd been looking forward to it enormously. My foster mother and I had fixed up my new, small house. It looked really cosy. On the day, my mother and I went there together, and it felt like a very festive day. Until the moment that she left me there. I'll never forget how I felt when she walked away from me. I was suddenly three years old again. I felt what it was like to be abandoned by my mother. It was as if the ground under my feet crumbled away. I had to say very directly to myself that it was different this time. My mother might have done that to me, but my foster mother never would. And I wasn't three any more, but 20. I wasn't a vulnerable little child. With the help of my friends and my foster parents, I could take care of myself.

Entering a lasting relationship

When (young) adults decide to live together or marry, they say farewell to an independent, 'free' life. For most people this is a big step which doesn't only bring feelings of happiness with it. Many people are, for a short time or a longer time, bothered with 'fear of commitment'. You give up your free life and don't yet know what you will get in return.

For adoptees and former foster children, this transition can be especially complicated, but it can also be a very empowering step:

in the end, you're attaching yourself again to someone you love. Sometimes there is additional uncertainty about the future: will you be able to keep this up? Will your partner be able to keep this up? Are you good enough? Fear of commitment or of abandonment can play a role in this. If a lasting relationship is eventually broken off, that usually has considerable influence on adult adoptees and foster children. Splitting up often brings to the surface the pain of rejection. Antonio (31), adopted from Bogotá, has this to say about it:[20]

> My greatest challenge has to do with romantic relationships. In my opinion that's where it goes wrong for every adopted child. Try finding the adoptee who isn't bothered by it at all. I haven't met anyone like that. Life forces you to acknowledge that. That's the scenario that you're acting out. If you look at the arguments I had with my parents and my brother, it often seemed as if it gripped me more than them. I think that the fear of a sort of conditional love was playing a role. We never really talked about it, but I think it's a feeling that my brother doesn't know. He's not adopted. I don't think he has that insecure feeling.

Having a baby

For most people, becoming a father or mother is one of the most profound experiences in their lives. This transitional process is so all-encompassing that it usually takes a few years before you've completely found your footing.

For adoptees and former foster children, there's an extra dimension to having a baby. Adoptees have a family member who is genetically linked to them for the first time in their life. Suddenly they're looking in a mirror: the baby has their eyes, their smile, their feet; often they experience a 'primal kinship' for the first time in their life. Olvi (31), from Indonesia, says this about having her first daughter:[21]

> At certain moments, I see myself in my daughter. That's new to me and so unbelievably beautiful. The feeling that there's no solid ground under you is gone.

San-Ho (42), from South Korea, says this about being a father:[22]

> I really wanted to have children. As an adopted child, it was a revelation for me to have children of my own. For most people, it's perfectly obvious to speak about what they've inherited from whom, but I never had anything from anyone. Now I can see myself in my three children. Wonderful!

After the birth of their child, some adopted and foster children suddenly feel a strong need to look for their birth parents. Tamara (40), who has a Russian–Austrian background, says this about the birth of her second child:[23]

> It might sound strange, but, for a woman, giving birth to a daughter is different from giving birth to a son. Different blood runs through the female line. I saw her and she was like a small babushka. In a flash, I saw all those generations of Russian women in her. I thought: you're here for a reason. You're here to take me back. Because of you, I can't deny it any longer.

Many adult foster children and adoptees are already confronted during their pregnancy with the feeling that their birth parents did not look after them properly. The pain of being placed in foster care or of being given up often takes on a whole new dimension; as a result, room has to be created once again for the past. Adoptee Mirjam (39) says this about the moment when her first child was born:[24]

> Anger began to take control of me. Anger directed against Pam [my birth mother]. I felt a new and powerful impulse to justify myself. My question was, again and again, how in heaven's name was it possible for her to give me up. Me, whom she carried under her heart for nine months, whom she felt inside, who she'd given life to.

While they're raising their child(ren), adult foster children often think back to their own childhood, when they were less well protected and carefree. The pain about that earlier, insecure situation and about the role of their original parents can have an influence on them. Hille (42), a foster child, says this:[25]

The idea that I was going to be a mother, was one that I had to get used to. The responsibility weighed heavily on me. I had to learn how to treat my child affectionately, because I'd never experienced it myself. For me, the word mother, being a mother, had always been associated with rejection. I struggled with that for a long time.

The death of a loved one

Adoptees and foster children are especially vulnerable to the death of a loved one. To be cut off forever from someone you love often triggers the old pain of the first separation. As a result, children and adolescents can experience strong feelings of loneliness, anxiety and abandonment. Former foster child Tim (25) tells about the death of his foster mother:

> I was nine years old when my foster mother died of breast cancer. After her death I was often afraid of being sent back to my own parents, but fortunately my foster father kept reassuring me that this wasn't going to happen.

> Oddly enough, I sometimes felt that my foster mother had failed me terribly. Deep within, I resented her for dying. I felt angry and lonely for a very long time. Just the same, in fact, as when I was placed in foster care. I think my reproaches had to do with that. My foster mother was supposed to protect me, but she had abandoned me, just like my own mother.

Sometimes the death of a parent can be a significant moment for closing a chapter. That's what former foster child Marilyn (53) says:

> My father was a victim of war. He never processed the trauma. But we could sense his powerlessness and his anger all the time and everywhere. It wounded us, sisters and brothers, for life. The acknowledgement of trauma is important, but that cannot happen if you never talk about it, like my father. It seemed as though he only partly existed. From the moment he died, I decided that I would do things differently. Death, which silenced my father forever, caused me to speak out. In that sense, his death was liberating for me.

Adult foster children and adoptees can experience intense sadness after the death of a birth parent because it means that they can no longer hope for a 'happy ending'. Foster child Joanne (36) says about the death of her mother:

> My mother had cancer. I remember visiting her. She was already very ill. I sat down next to her and took her hand. But she pushed me away. I was rejected once more. I began to boil deep inside. I got up and left the room uttering oaths. She died the same night. I would never be able to go back to her. That was a huge slap in the face. It could never be put right. I think that's the thing that has caused me the most pain in my life.

Abortion

Women and men who decide to have an abortion often carry this unborn child in their hearts for the rest of their lives. For adoptees and foster children, having an abortion can be even more intense. Former foster child Marianne (31) says:

> When my friend and I decided to have an abortion, we were sure that it was the right decision. We were too young, we still had to finish our education and neither of us had a proper job yet. It was a difficult decision, but we were still able to make it quite easily. It was only a few years later, when we actually wanted a child, that it started to bother me. I quickly became pregnant again, but I kept thinking of that first baby that we had had aborted. Why had we done it? The rational arguments that we'd found so convincing didn't make sense any more. I began to wonder if I was cut out to be a good parent. In fact, I was just as unscrupulous as my birth mother. I hadn't given my own child a chance for a life with us. Why hadn't I thought of that then? It caused me enormous pain. Who was I, really, if I could make such a rational decision? I couldn't get rid of a feeling of shame, even after I'd given birth to a beautiful, healthy daughter. It was only after a few more years that I was able to come to terms with the abortion, with the help of a social worker. I told her about my feelings of shame and guilt. In the end, I learned that I needed to make room in my heart for the

child that couldn't stay. I've made a diary for my dreams and wishes for her. By means of that book, she has a loving and visible place in our hearts and our lives. Even my four-year-old daughter knows about her missing sister. We talk about it sometimes and imagine what it would be like for her to have an older sister. Sometimes that hurts, but it helps too. You can't hide something like that away. Our unborn child belongs with us too, forever.

If an adoptee or foster child loses a child through a miscarriage or stillbirth, they can also experience deep sadness. The longing for a blood relationship is usually strong, so this often causes extra pain.

Unfulfilled desire to have a baby

Unwanted childlessness can cause an intense grieving process to adult adopted and foster children. The longing 'to do better than the birth parents' cannot be fulfilled. It often also means that a powerful desire to have a genetic relationship has to be abandoned. Adoptee Christianne (35) says:

> When I found out that I would never be able to have a child of my own, my world collapsed. I wept intensely for days. I thought that my tears would never stop. What hit me most was that I had always dreamt about having my own child, about bringing someone into the world who looked like me. This primal connection was something I would never experience and the pain that it caused was beyond words. I wouldn't have a chance to create a new family line with my genes. I felt intensely lonely and wept about my adoption and about everything that had happened in my life. And about having to give up my dearest dream, a child that would be born from my own womb. I'd never get the chance to 'make up' for my own childhood. I couldn't make it worthwhile by doing a better job myself.

Adopted child Indah (45), from Indonesia, says:

> I'd always had a dream that I would make a new beginning; I didn't know my parents, but I would pass my genes on to a new generation, and that generation would produce another generation. In my imagination, a whole new family would come into existence.

But suddenly I was 42 and I still hadn't managed to become pregnant. I had to accept that I would never experience a genetic connection with my children. And then the need gradually grew in me to search for unknown members of my family. There had to be someone in the world that I could feel a primal connection with.

There are many life-cycle losses that can touch upon the core loss. Losing a job, for example, or moving house, failing an exam, having your house broken into or being robbed – all of these things can trigger the feelings of loss associated with adoption or being placed in foster care. How you deal with these losses depends on, among other things, your history, your nature/abilities and your environment. In order to be better able to understand your feelings, it can be helpful to learn to recognise the connection between certain losses.

Factors that hinder the mourning process

'Healthy ways to mourn' means, among other things, that you dare to feel the pain that comes from having suffered a loss and that, after a period of time, you also dare to connect with both the positive and the negative aspects of that loss. In order to go through such a process, you need *strength* and *basic trust*; you also need an environment that gives you *support*. For adopted and foster children, the presence of these elements doesn't go without saying. In the pages below, I will identify a number of areas of vulnerability that you might encounter as a result of your history. It might be that, as a result of one or more of these themes, you are unable to achieve a full mourning process. If that is the case, then you should seek the help of a specialist care-giver in the grieving process.

Diminished stress regulation

If at a very young age you were neglected or undernourished or if your mother was addicted to alcohol or drugs during pregnancy, this will have had a significant influence on the development of your brain. There is then a very good chance that your stress regulation system is pitched to a more sensitive level, as a result of which you might find it difficult to deal with stress and with intense emotions. You may therefore prefer to avoid stressful situations. For the same reason you might avoid feelings of pain and sadness; possibly you are afraid that these feelings will overwhelm you. As a result you might not be able to grieve about your losses. (See also sections 'The body and body awareness: reducing stress' on p.76 and 'The heart: making room for pain' on p.84)

Insufficient basic trust

Foster children and adoptees might suffer from a lack of basic trust to a greater or lesser degree. Basic trust can be described as:

> The trust that you have in yourself and your surroundings. The trust that your feelings and thoughts are allowed, and that you know deep inside that your parents or carers, your friends, your colleagues won't reject you if you are angry sometimes or make a mistake.

In order to deal with the pain of a significant loss, it's important that you've been able to build up sufficient basic trust. Without basic trust, you won't be able to regulate your emotions, and you won't, then, dare to fully experience the pain; nor will you feel secure enough with your tutors or your friends to show your emotions. Possibly you will be afraid that they will not support you, and that support is something that you need very badly in a grieving process. Foster child Els (46) tells, for example, how she decided as a three-and-a-half-year-old not to let anyone close to her feelings:[26]

> If someone came in to look at me, I would pretend to be sleeping. Nobody but nobody was going to see that I was crying or sad. It was my secret, because I was going to be strong and tough, strong and tough. And I was going to keep that up for my whole life, but I didn't know it at the time. One day I realised: my parents are not going to come and get me; I'm going to have to do it all on my own in this life. So I bore my fate proudly and held my curly head up high. And I decided that I would let no one, absolutely no one, get close to my heart.

Whether or not you have been able to establish basic trust does not only depend on the way you were raised by your carers, adoptive or foster parents. Some children have experienced too much and are therefore unable to completely trust themselves and others. There are also children who have experienced a great deal, but who seem to have so much resilience that they are still able to establish basic trust to some extent. It depends, then, on your nature and constitution.

If you regularly experience difficulties – for example, in your relationships, your work or education, then it is possible that you have not (yet) built up sufficient basic trust.

Postponed, accumulated and complex grieving

Children who suffer a significant loss often postpone mourning it until adulthood. This can have a variety of causes. (See section 'Three factors that influence the mourning process' on p.33.) Often the pain only surfaces with the appearance of a new loss. This is often the case with foster children and adoptees. Their carers then sometimes fail to recognise the pain of the core loss because it happened so long ago. Daniel (24), adopted from Columbia, tells how complicated it can be to get close to your core loss:[27]

> After a long time, the realisation began to force its way onto me that my problems probably had something to do with my adoption. This is a big step, because it means that a breach has been made in the denial mechanism. At first I sought help because I felt lonely and I wasn't able to get close to anyone. I've since come to understand that deeper causes are underlying this problem. The feeling of loss in particular plays a large role in my life and in all of the relationships that I attempt to build up […].

He tells later how important it can be to mourn your core loss:

> Depression can be caused by an incomplete grieving process. Some adopted children speak about a deep-rooted sadness that seems to be relentless and intrusive, an obstacle to real pleasure.

If someone postpones grieving over several losses in his life, then he's left with subsurface smouldering peat fires. One speaks then about *accumulated grief* (see section 'Postponed, accumulated and complicated grief' on p.28). Many adult foster children and adoptees experience this, especially if they have not learned how to deal with their losses in a constructive way during their youth. It then becomes difficult to grieve for all of these losses in adulthood. It is possible as a result to develop *complicated grief*; in that case, it is necessary to seek the help of an experienced grief therapist.

Former foster child David (30) only began to process his many feelings of loss in adulthood. By accumulating all of the losses from his youth, he ended up with depression:[28]

> I'm now 30 and if I look back on my childhood, I think that I've ended up OK. If you've had a turbulent youth, you are forced to grow up quickly. This gave me the advantage that by the time that I was 18 my life was on its way. I had quickly gotten a good job and was settled. Nevertheless, two years ago I found myself struggling with depression. I thought I had my life well organised, but I found it difficult to deal with my emotions and to form relationships with people [...]. I worked intensively with a therapist to get out of my depression.

Unprocessed traumatic experiences

Foster and adopted children have often experienced traumatic losses in their childhood. If you still haven't been able to fully process this, it can disturb the mourning process. It's possible that you have not been able to defuse certain traumatic losses because they were too intense – for example, if you've been raped, mistreated, abused, if you've been a witness to mistreatment or if you've experienced war, fire, natural disaster or an accident. The fact that you were abandoned or neglected as a child can also have been experienced as a traumatic loss. The loss is then imprinted on your senses. Adopted and foster children often carry with them such unconscious memories. The older you get, the more difficult it can be to come into contact with those memories.

Trauma can usually be effectively treated with *EMDR* ('Eye Movement Desensitisation and Reprocessing'), *counselling* and *writing therapy*; a combination of these often works well.

Sensorimotor psychotherapy is also effective in cases of trauma. This type of therapy works with the body's memories and makes use of movement and Mindfulness techniques to integrate the trauma, so you don't constantly have to re-experience the past. In addition, it is possible to come into contact with early memories by means of 'Guided Affective Imagery'. If a traumatic memory is effectively treated, it is possible to neutralise or normalise the feelings and thoughts about the experience. The fear that is associated with an experience partly disappears, which makes it easier to take steps in the mourning process. In the Further Reading section, there are a number of books about trauma in children and adults which might be of additional help. You can read more about EMDR at www.emdr.com. You can read more about sensorimotor therapy at www.sensorimotorpsychotherapy.org. At both of these websites you can find therapists specialising in these kinds of treatment. It is important in any case that you seek the advice of a specialist in cases of unprocessed trauma.

The inability to achieve closure

Adoptees and former foster children often cannot achieve closure for their core loss. That means that they often cannot leave their past behind them and cannot form a new relationship with whom or what they have lost. Some grieve their entire lives because they are missing important parts of their life story. Others mourn for years because they have a complicated relationship with their birth parents – for example, if they are very unpredictable in their expressions of affection. Foster child Emily (50) says:

> I never really trusted my parents in their responses towards me. We had a visitation agreement, but I never knew how such a weekend would unfold. One time they'd be sweet and would have bought presents for us, and another time they'd be unfriendly and refused even to smile. In fact, that's how my relationship with my father continued to be. Even four years ago, when he was on his death bed, I was on my guard, and for good reason as it happened: an hour before he died, he made a foul comment. I think that all the times that I was rejected and then approached again caused

me the most pain. I'm glad that this struggle is finally over. It was a constant theme of my life.

Many adoptees and foster children don't know whether they'll ever meet family members. If you're still young, it can be quite nice to fantasise about your birth family; it can appease a longing for 'wholeness' and give you the hope that you will meet them one day. But that hope could also turn out to be a false one, or the final meeting might be disappointing. The aftermath of a meeting can also be complicated, especially because it is often unclear then how the relationship will develop. Your birth parents may be in trouble, and you feel torn apart. You might experience feelings of guilt, or be fearful about a new rejection, now or in the future. Adopted/foster child Els (46) tells about a difficult meeting with her mother:[29]

> The pain in my heart has remained and it flares up at unexpected moments. Despite everything, I love her very much. I spent so little time thinking about her in the past, and I spend so much time thinking about her now. Maybe I had some catching up to do? But the illusion that I had that one day I could leave it all behind, that's completely gone. My adoption and my relationship with her is a part of my life. It's a part of me.

Grieving about 'what might have been' can be a life-long theme, even if you've have bonded well with your carers, your adoptive or foster family. It can be helpful to make use of farewell rituals at significant moments, so that certain periods or moments can be marked in a symbolic way (see section 'The present: saying farewell and giving meaning' on p.98).

Questions
Knowledge questions

1. What feelings of pain and longing can you experience during your life as a result of being adopted or placed in foster care? Name five.

2. Denial sometimes works as a protection mechanism. Give, for each age group, two reasons why denial can be helpful:

- in children

- in teenagers/adolescents

- in adults.

3. When is denial no longer functional? Give an example.

4. What is postponed grief? Why do children often postpone grieving? Give three reasons.

5. Why is it important that you grieve about the core loss? What can happen when new losses occur?

6. Many adoptees and foster children do not dare to process their feelings of pain. Why?

7. What is basic trust? What influence can the degree of basic trust have on the process of grieving?

8. If you are unable to say farewell to someone or something, this can hinder the process of grieving. Explain why.

PERSONAL QUESTIONS

1. What feelings of pain and longing about the core loss did/do you have to deal with:

- as a child

- as a teenager/adolescent

- as an adult?

2. What life losses have you experienced during your life? Which of those losses are most strongly associated with your feelings about your core loss?

CHAPTER 3

The Circle of Connecting
Coping with Loss

Seven connecting themes

Mourning is a process involving connecting and letting go. In some periods you may feel the need to connect with the pain; at other moments you may need to let go of the pain and to think about the present and the future. These two movements in the process of mourning are equally important: in order to keep your balance, you need both constructive-orientated moments and loss-orientated moments. In the Circle of Connecting, which I have developed especially for adoptees and foster children, I show you how you can give attention to both movements. The Circle is applicable to core losses, but also to other life losses.

In the Circle, seven fundamental elements are central: the body, the mind, the heart, the environment, the past, the present and the future. Both children and adults can identify with these elements. Depending on your needs, you can be loss-orientated at one moment and constructive-orientated at another. At important moments of transition in your life, you might be directly concerned with feelings of loss, while during other periods you might prefer to be connected with the present or the future.

Although the Circle has no predetermined route and no beginning or end, I have given the body a central place in the Circle of Connecting. In my opinion, the body has an extremely important function in dealing with loss: the degree to which you are aware of your body and to which you keep your body in shape, well cared for and well fed has a great influence on how you feel. Also the rhythm of your heartbeat and the pattern of your breathing has a large influence on how you experience things. By being more aware of your body and connecting with it, you can take important steps forward in the process of mourning.

As an extension to being aware of your body, 'Mindfulness' and 'Acceptance and Commitment Theory' will be addressed later in the Circle; they are both new currents in Western psychology, based on the assumption that not all problems in life have to be solved. Mindfulness has to do especially with awareness of the body and living in the present; that helps you to put your thoughts and feelings in perspective and feel more at ease. Acceptance and Commitment Theory is also concerned with this body awareness, but then goes a step further. If we can accept that not all problems have to be solved, then we can finally connect with our deepest values and live in accordance with them. The solution might be to accept our problems and commit ourselves to the purest fire of life that burns within us. Problems are, after all, part of life. Daniël, adopted from Columbia, refers us to Nietzsche on this point:[30]

> If we can believe Nietzsche, our human existence brings with it something that is unavoidable. The problems which are part of our human nature will keep coming back. So we shouldn't hope to find happiness in solving or freeing ourselves from the problems. They give our whole existence its meaning. Without problems, our lives would be threatened by the second most serious thing – boredom, that is. We ought to learn to see our problems as a challenge and accept them cheerfully. By seeking creative solutions each time, we can experience the greatest happiness.

I developed the Circle of Connecting as there are so many different ways to mourn and because mourning in fact has no beginning and no end; you can make use of it in your own way and draw from it your entire life. It doesn't matter in what order you look at it, or how many themes you choose to investigate more deeply. Each and every one of them can be an important source of healing. For all of the themes, additional literature is recommended. You can find these titles (organised according to theme) at the back of the book. I haven't attempted to be exhaustive with this list of sources, but I expect that it will put you on a path that you can pursue on your own.

I am convinced that every person is an expert on himself, and that every person knows, deep inside, what he needs. In following (parts of) the Circle, keep in mind the 'factors that hinder the mourning process' (see section on p.66) and ask for the help of a specialist if you feel the need.

The Circle of Connecting

In the Circle of Connecting, you will be put in touch with one or more of the seven themes; you choose the elements that you want to connect with at that moment: your body, your mind, your heart, your environment, your past, present or future. By frequently making contact with (one of) the themes in the Circle, you are connecting with yourself, with your history and with what has happened to you. The seven themes can help you to give what has happened to you a different perspective and to have new feelings and thoughts about it. Working with the seven themes can encourage you to a greater acceptance of what has happened or to make more sense of it. By alternately being busy with your losses in a more loss-orientated or more constructive-orientated way, it might be possible for you to reconnect with the past, present and future and to better form a new bond with what you've lost.

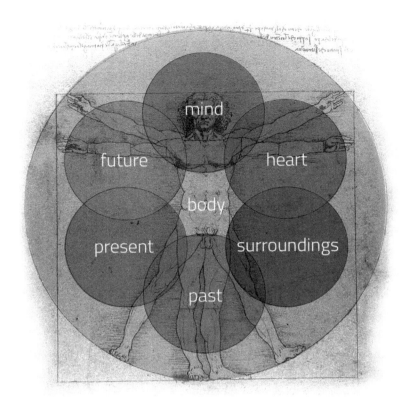

Figure 3.1 The Circle of Connecting

The body and body awareness: reducing stress

When you mourn, it is important to connect with your body. You can do this by taking good care of your body and by developing body awareness. This will allow the stress response of your nervous system to function better, and that is important during times of stress. Dr Servan Schreiber (2003) describes a number of effective and simple methods for tapping your physical energy sources; his methods can easily be adapted to everyday life. I summarise, below, the most important energy sources. I also briefly discuss the importance of attention/body awareness.

PHYSICAL EXERCISE, DAYLIGHT AND NOURISHMENT
Physical exercise protects you from too much anxiety, despair and depression. A great deal of research has been published about this.

This is because if you get enough exercise, your brain produces more endorphins, chemicals that have more or less the same effect on your emotional brain as opium or morphine; you feel more content and alert right away. According to Schreiber, opium is actually the strongest antidote in existence against the pain caused by separation or mourning.[31] Endorphins have more or less the same effect. So people who exercise regularly can often cope better with a setback. It also strengthens your immune system.

Natural light is also an important energy-enhancer. It reaches the brain through the eyes and is passed on to the hypothalamus; this is the part of the brain that is located in the heart of the emotional brain. It regulates, among other things, the appetite, libido, body temperature, the metabolism of fats, the sleeping and menstrual cycles. The hypothalamus also regulates our moods and the energy with which we engage in relationships. Someone who gets too little daylight can develop a variety of complaints and can also become gloomy and passive. Light, then, influences the exchange of energy between your body and your brain. During times of stress, it can help if you expose yourself to as much daylight as possible.

Finally, healthy foods can also enhance your energy. There is now scientific evidence that diet has an influence on almost all major Western diseases, including cancer, heart and circulatory diseases. But a healthy diet doesn't only influence your body, it also influences the condition of your brain. Someone who follows a 'Mediterranean' diet, for example, with a good deal of vegetable fats and fish, takes in many more healthy fats and vitamins; these go directly to the membranes of the brain and transform, according to Servan-Schreiber (2005), its structure. If you eat more complex, unsaturated fatty-acids (the fats that are fluid at room temperature), then the shell of the brain cells becomes softer and more supple, and communication between cells stabilises. You're less troubled, then, with gloominess, anxiety and insomnia. You also get more energy. In addition, essential fatty-acids, such as omega 3, enhance the variability of your heart rhythms, something that can also protect you from depression.[32] So a healthy diet is not only good for your heart, but also good for your brain.

BODY AWARENESS/MINDFULNESS

Emotions always produce a reaction in our bodies. As soon as we experience a strong emotion, for example, our heart, begins to beat more quickly and irregularly. The rapid, irregular heart beat can often mean that we are no longer fully aware of our surroundings and ourselves; we experience a tunnelled, limited reality. It often feels, then, as if you are 'overwhelmed with emotions'. Because of the tunnelling, your self-image and your feelings merge, even though that's not the reality, because you are much more than that one feeling.

If you learn to involve your five senses (smell, touch, sight, taste and hearing) much more in your experience, you probably won't be overwhelmed by your feelings during emotional moments; that can help to reduce stress. 'Being mindful' is something that everyone can learn; it has to do with a more attentive awareness of your body and of the here and now with all of your senses. If you involve all five senses in your experience, you can keep calmer, be less constrained and experience a situation as less 'absolute'. You can find out for yourself how 'mindful' you are by nature by asking yourself these questions:

- Are you consciously aware of your surroundings during a long walk or a cycling trip?

- Do you have a strong preference for a visual (sight), auditory (hearing) or kinaesthetic (touch) learning strategy? Can you combine the three?

- Are you aware of the flow of water when you're showering? Are you aware of what the shower does to your body?

- Can you put things in perspective, or do you often think in terms of 'absolutes', such as never or always?

- If you become totally involved in something, are you then still aware of your body and your surroundings?

- When you are playing a sport, are you able to be in the here and now, involved in the movement, or are you focused on reaching your goal above all?

- Can you listen to others without judging, or are you usually busy with your own response to what you're being told?

- Can you be aware of the here and now, or are you usually busy in your head with what's coming next?

There are many practical books available for children and adults which can teach you to be 'mindful'. In the list of titles at the back of the book, I make some suggestions. Most of these books contain exercises (see Further Reading list).

BREATHING/HEART COHERENCE
If you are more aware of your breathing, you can experience more physical and emotional peace. There are twice as many nerve connections between the emotional brain and the heart, as there are between the emotional brain and the cognitive (rational) brain; so if your heart begins to beat more rapidly, then that has a much greater effect on how you feel than on how you think. If people experience too many emotions, they often get a feeling of being 'overwhelmed'. That's true in one sese because if you experience too many emotions, then your cognitive and emotional brain don't work well together: the nerve connections give more nourishment to your emotional brain. That may give you the feeling that you 'are your emotions', and that you merge with them.

Your cognitive and emotional brain work best together when they are in balance with each other. You achieve this if your heart beat has a regular, coherent rhythm. This is not necessarily the same as a 'calm rhythm'; a regular, coherent rhythm can be intense at the same time. If you breathe with more awareness, then you create 'cardiac coherence'. You will then experience 'flow': head and heart work together well. When there is this physiological balance, you will be better able to feel emotions without being overwhelmed by them. That can be very helpful during times of mourning or stress. In addition, you'll preserve a lot more energy if you experience physiological balance. In that way you'll tap a very useful source of energy.

Most people are familiar with the feeling of 'flow' because our heartbeat is in coherence when we are experiencing positive emotions such as love, gratitude and compassion. A work of art, then, or beautiful music can generate cardiac coherence, as can a walk through a natural landscape, a hobby, love for your child, partner or dog, furnishing your house or the first day of spring. Religion, spiritual life, yoga or meditation can also create physiological balance. We then find ourselves in a moment of 'flow'; our breathing is coherent and it brings our body and brain into balance, with the result that we can look at the world in a clear and nuanced way.

In the Further Reading list at the back of the book, there are a number of books and websites about cardiac coherence and breathing. Books about mindfulness also devote attention to breathing.

The mind: knowing your inner beliefs and thoughts

Inner beliefs and thoughts determine to a large extent how we feel and how we deal with a loss. For that reason it's important to connect with your 'mind'; by identifying your thoughts or beliefs, you can find out whether they are helping you with the mourning process or in fact are working against you. Whether you have coping thoughts or thoughts that work against you depends to some extent on your character. One person is by nature more optimistic and resilient than another. But the way that you think about yourself or about the things that happen to you also depends in part on how much basic trust you've been able to develop and on your upbringing. If your parents or carers were always open and sensitive and if there was ample room for emotions, it is more likely that you have developed an open and positive state of mind and that you find emotions 'quite normal' and take them seriously. Your parents' beliefs and expectations are usually anchored unconsciously in your personality.

They might have told you that 'big boys don't cry'. The statement that 'you always make a mountain out of a molehill' might also have been passed on to you, or that you're a 'nag', that you 'don't need anyone' or 'that you should be grateful just to be here'; that might be a reason not to take your sadness seriously (any more) when you're an adult.

Your adoption or history of placement has probably also had an influence on your thoughts and beliefs. If you were neglected or abandoned in childhood, you might have developed the belief 'that you don't need anyone', 'that you can't trust anyone' or 'that you're not worth the trouble'. Foster child Els (42) says this:[33]

> What's stayed with me the most is that I've locked myself up like a tomb; I didn't let anyone see who I really was; nobody was going to put me down, that was what I kept telling myself. I was strong and tough, tough and strong.

Statements or thoughts like these are often helpful when someone is young: they protect a child against feeling too much pain or they help to adjust to new surroundings, in order to survive. By having these thoughts, a child can function on his own or can get love and positive attention from his carers and/or his friends at school. In that sense, feelings of guilt and shame and feelings of control and power ('I've got everything under control') can be helpful at some time; in any case, for as long as it takes to bond with the new carers. But once a child has developed sufficient basic trust or has become an adult, such thoughts have become automatic and may no longer be helping. In fact, they can work against you. They can disturb the mourning process or even prevent you from beginning to mourn. Mirjam (39), who was adopted, says this:[34]

> On the basis of those feelings and the damaging ideas [that I had no right to live], I began to react and I had spun a web of lies around myself. Without realising it, I'd placed myself under all sorts of commandments and prohibitions. 'I wasn't allowed to be there', 'I wasn't allowed to be happy', 'I wasn't supposed to be fun' – I can list a lot more.

Inner beliefs, then, say something about your history and about your upbringing. But they also say something about you. You experienced it this way (your sister or brother probably developed other beliefs) and you created this 'truth' out of it. It can be very worthwhile to identify your inner beliefs or automatic thoughts and to ask yourself whether they are still appropriate for you or whether you want to replace them with new, coping statements.

Negative automatic thoughts or beliefs that might block the mourning process include:

- 'I have to do everything by myself after all.'

- 'I have everything under control/I can take care of myself very well.'

- 'My birth father wasn't a good person, I certainly will not mourn him.'

- 'My mother should have protected me when I was small. I'll never get over this.'

- 'I'm so ashamed of my past; I will never tell anyone about it.'

- 'It's all because of the adoption/because of the foster placement.'

- 'I have to be grateful for being here and I cannot be angry.'

This last statement has probably been formed by the 'outside world'. But by hearing from the people around you again and again that you're not allowed to be angry, you're left stewing in anger. Jennifer (22) from Columbia says:

> I'm still very angry with my birth father. First he mistreated my mother and then he abandoned both of us. That's not normal, is it? But if I tell that to people around me, they always try to soothe my anger. Then they say: 'Just leave it alone; you have good contact with your birth mother, that's really lovely.' Or they say: 'You have a good life and you have kind adoptive parents; if you'd stayed with your mother, you would have been a lot worse off.'

Then I just get angrier. Society thinks I shouldn't complain. I've got it good. But I have a right to be angry with my father. It's not normal, is it, that you mistreat your wife and then you just let your wife and child drop dead?

If you feel the need, during the mourning process, to connect with the past (section 'The past: searching for pieces to the puzzle' on p.88), certain automatic thoughts or beliefs can block your desire to search for information. Negative, automatic thoughts include:

- 'I won't find anything anyway.'

- 'Nobody is waiting for me to show up.'

- 'My birth mother is undoubtedly still addicted/depressed/rejecting.'

- 'No matter what I find, the information won't be correct.'

- 'I'm not going to search; I can't deal with those emotions.'

Both children and adults can learn to replace negative, automatic thoughts that aren't helpful with coping statements or thoughts. Identify them and investigate them by asking yourself questions such as:

- How did this notion come into being? What purpose did it serve?

- Is the earlier purpose still helpful/functional?

- How realistic are my thoughts about this?

- How realistic are the thoughts of the 'outside world' about this? What can I do to make sure that I'm less bothered by them?

- Can I look at this in a more nuanced way?

- How do I feel when I'm thinking those thoughts?

- Do those thoughts still fit me?

- How can I transform these thoughts/convictions into constructive thoughts that do help me?

There are always *possibilities* in coping thoughts, while there aren't in negative thoughts. When you learn to judge the world and your situation more realistically, there's a good chance that you'll begin to experience your history in a more nuanced way. In the section 'The body and body awareness: reducing stress' (p.76), I described the importance of body awareness and mindfulness. When you're able to experience more than just your one feeling or thought, it can help you cope better. It also helps to look at the 'beliefs of the outside world' in a more nuanced way. It's not usually possible to change the beliefs in your surroundings, no matter how often you try. Which beliefs in you cause you to become angry or sad again and again? You might think over and over that 'No one understands me; I'm all alone'; or you might think: 'You see: everybody's out to hurt me.' You might question such negative, automatic thoughts or beliefs as I've indicated above. Often they arise as reflexes without conscious deliberation. You can't change the world, but you can change yourself.

In the Further Reading list at the back of the book, you can find suggestions for reading that can help you to investigate your negative, automatic thoughts and change them. These books are all based on Rational Emotive Behavior Therapy (REBT).

The heart: making room for pain

For many people, connecting with the heart (symbol for your feelings) is not easy. Especially when feelings are powerful, we are often afraid of losing control over the mind and the body. For adoptees and foster children, it is often even more difficult to deal with powerful feelings. This is partly because the *stress regulation of their nervous system* is often functioning more sensitively, especially when they have received little or no comfort from their carers during the first years of their life – for example, when they were hungry, had a stomach ache or were stressed. They weren't touched so often, cuddled or fed and therefore, repeatedly, their emotional brain was not soothed in a natural way. As a result, many adoptees and foster children have developed an overactive stress response. Often, in adulthood, they still do not dare to feel emotions such as anger, sadness, fear and joy: they have the feeling that they can't regulate such feelings effectively, and in a sense that's right: they haven't learned how to do so well enough as a baby. In that way you can develop the feeling that 'you'll lose yourself if you really release your feelings'. But in fact you don't lose 'yourself' by releasing powerful emotions: you lose control over your body (increased heartbeat and rapid breathing) and your mind; your emotions take over because your heart is beating faster and pumping more blood to your emotional brain than to your cognitive brain.

It is still important to make contact with the pain that is buried in your heart. You can defuse the feelings of pain, then, which will allow you to experience more peace and quiet. If you succeed in *not judging your feelings* and if you dare to look at them *kindly and with acceptance*, then you can make better contact with your heart. That means that you stop struggling against your feelings, and that the feelings can 'just' be there. Emmy (40), who was adopted, says:[35]

> I sat [beside my adoptive mother's deathbed] and asked myself whether I was allowed to feel sad. I wasn't sure. If I now, as a child, feel really sad, am I being disloyal to my birth mother? I was being blocked by my feelings of loyalty. I talked about it with my brothers and sisters and asked them if it was OK for me to feel sad. They said that I had a right to feel sad. Later I sat beside my adoptive mother's deathbed and I realised that I was sad for her, but also for my birth mother; these feelings could co-exist. […] It was suddenly clear to me that if I could feel sad for both of them, I could also love both of them. I realised that I was happy that I had grown up in that adoptive family and that I am also happy with my birth mother.

Someone who dares to create room for pain can also release intense anger, shame or guilt. Pain is usually hiding beneath those strong feelings, and the pain deserves to be acknowledged. If you can make room for the pain, you can feel more at peace. This is what adoptee Mirjam (39) says when she's had her first child:[36]

> Anger began to take control of me. Anger directed at Pam [my birth mother]. I found a new drive, in which I could justify myself. My question was, again and again, how was it possible to abandon me? Me, whom she carried for nine months beneath her heart, who she felt, to whom she gave life. But it felt as if I kept failing to get an answer, so I keep going with my resentment. Finally, Pam wisely stops responding.

> I kept working on this process, with all the sadness, anger, powerlessness and pain in me. Letters to Pam that I never sent. But, for me, it was such a relief to make room for all these feelings. Paper always agrees with you. That's what I needed. I was right, it was my feeling, I was abandoned, I was treated unjustly.

In the section 'The body and body awareness: reducing stress' (p.76), I've indicated how, with the help of *mindfulness and body awareness*, you can achieve more calmness in experiencing emotions. In fact, you throw an 'anchor' out: the boat of your feelings, which has been tossing about in a storm, has something to hold on to, an anchor in the here and now. In order to learn this, you can take a course in mindfulness or read a book about it and do exercises on your own (see Further Reading list).

You can also make use of *breathing techniques* in order to avoid being overwhelmed by your feelings. Then your body, your emotional brain and cognitive brain keep communicating with each other. In the Further Reading list you can find some helpful books about heart coherence and breathing techniques that can help you on the way (see Further Reading). You can also exercise with breathing techniques in a mindfulness, meditation or yoga class.

The surroundings: seeking support

In periods of mourning, 'connecting with your surroundings' is an important theme; getting support is one of the most important stress-reducing factors. Support can come from friends, family, a care-provider, a neighbour, or someone in the same position. Getting support can have a number of functions:

- It can be *comforting*: you have the feeling that you're not in it alone.

- It can be *a relief*: 'putting everything out there' helps with your emotion and stress regulation.

- It can give *insight*: you can express your feelings and thoughts and someone else can respond to them. This makes it possible for you to reflect and, in a sense, look at your own story in a mirror. In addition, having someone else look at your situation can put things in perspective; it means that you can look at what's happened to you from different points of view.

Joelle (38), a former foster child, says:

> When my birth mother died, I got the most support from the woman who lived next door. She came by every morning at 11:00 for a cup of coffee, so we started the day together. That helped me so much. There are so many people who want to help and that was really valuable to me, but the most basic thing was that simple fact that every day my neighbour was there for me.

Former foster child Manuel (27) tells about the important role of his mentor at secondary school:

> There were lots of people who wanted to help me through puberty, but the most important thing for me was the conversations I had with my mentor at school. He was really a wonderful guy; I could always go to him. I stood there with him so many times raging and fuming, but he stayed calm and always let me be myself. I remember that I even called him once in the middle of the night because something was up. It was never too much for him. He was my saviour in need. Without him, my puberty would have been very different.

Many adoptees and foster children find it helpful to have one or more people in the same situation around them. You can look specifically for an association for adoptees or foster children, or you can make contact with people via social media, Yahoo or

Google groups and internet forums. If you join a support group or association, you may come into contact with all sorts of adoption and foster care themes that you find important and to which you want to devote some energy. In that way, you can to some extent give meaning to what has happened to you. Anand (36), an adopted child from Bombay says:[37]

> At that time, I became the chairperson of Kiran, the association of adopted children from India. The contact with other adoptees gave me some recognition. I can still remember that my parents thought it was odd: suddenly there were all these dark-skinned people at my birthday parties. It was especially a social activity club and I organised all sorts of activities. The club has since ceased to exist and I'm now active in UAI, *United Adoptees International*. There we are much busier with substantive questions about adoption. For example, we're trying to get the Indian government to the point that adopted children can have control over their own files.

The past: searching for pieces to the puzzle

For most foster children and adoptees, a part of their life story is missing. Searching for the missing parts can be an important element in the process of mourning. In that way, you integrate the pieces of your life story. Over the long term, this can give you more peace of mind; worries, questions, feelings of guilt or anxieties can be made visible and processed. Each piece of the puzzle can help you to shed new light on your adoption or foster placement. Liesbeth List (72), adopted in the Netherlands, says:[38]

> One day, my aunt gave me a pile of letters and other documents from my parents. Among them was my mother's death certificate, mentioning that she had taken her own life. No one had ever told me that. I was shattered: she had abandoned me, too. Unimaginable. I was in deep mourning for two weeks, until I could think more clearly again. I asked myself: why did my father give me up? Then I answered it myself: he came out of the war completely broken, gets his family back and then his wife commits suicide. He meets another woman and she treats his child very strangely.

He must have thought: this is only going to get worse. Getting rid of the woman wasn't an option, there were five other children by this other woman. So I had to go. By giving me up, he saved me. When I realised that, I could forgive my father. But there was also my mother's suicide. How can a woman take her life when she has a child to take care of? The only answer can be that she was completely shattered. I have heard what it was like in the Japanese camps: nothing to eat and violence everywhere. People went completely insane, and attacked each other. My mother had every right to commit suicide, but she did make sure that I was safe with my father.

GATHERING INFORMATION

You can gather information by investigating your adoption or youth care file. You can also request your birth certificate or police reports, which might contain useful information. Sometimes you can find out more about your past from relatives – for example, because they still have letters or other significant documents.

You might be confronted, during your search, with facts that are very different from what you had hoped to find. Your mother turns out to be ill or to have committed suicide; your parents don't want to meet you, or you don't get along at all; your family is very poor or has had a very difficult time; you discover that you are a child of incest. You can then be confronted with intense pain. In fact, you are mourning for what could not be: a valuable meeting, a good connection, a life with each other or a spark of hope of finding some meaningful memories. That can be a real blow. Ellis (45), adopted in the Netherlands, needs time to process the sad information that she finds about her mother:[39]

I heard that my mother died from carbon monoxide poisoning. She went to take a shower and had closed everything off. For me, the question whether it was an accident or suicide was very heavy, because you wouldn't leave your child behind uncared for! It's a thought that I cannot deal with. I am well aware that it was her reality and would seem different looking back. I could put it aside at the time. […] But it remains a sad and painful story. I also know that she didn't have an easy time of it. Being a mother really got to her deeply. It was something very intense for her.

Former foster child Samantha (31) is confronted with great sadness when she sees the youth welfare report. Suddenly there's the story about her childhood again, which now, as an adult, she looks at with very different eyes:

> Recently I read the investigation and reports about my childhood. It was more of a shock to me than I had expected. Suddenly the intense family situation in which I found myself became visible and tangible again. My mother had made two attempts at suicide. I found her both times. When I was a child, I just 'dealt' with it, but now, when I was confronted with it again, I was overwhelmed with intense sadness and pain. Suddenly I saw myself as a 12-year-old girl. How very tragic. My friends were busy with make-up and fantasising about their first boyfriends, and I was there at home and had to make sure that my mother didn't make another attempt at suicide.

Even if you've suffered a traumatic loss, it can be helpful to search for details. As long as you don't know the important facts, you keep thinking about it without conscious deliberation and a disquiet remains that can manifest itself in your life at any moment. If you know the facts about a traumatic event, you often are in better shape to mourn and let go.

GIVING A DNA SAMPLE

If you can't locate any information, you might be able to acquire valuable information about your past by means of a DNA test. Your DNA can contain information about the region where you originally came from and about the ethnic group that you belong to. It can even put you into contact with distant family members who are also looking for relatives with the help of a DNA test.

Jeroen (32), from Indonesia, discovered an important piece to his puzzle in that way. He had three tests done, and found out where his roots are. He says:[40]

> [The DNA tests show that I am] very likely to be an ordinary Indonesian. When my adoptive parents came to get me, it was suggested that my father is Chinese. But that is very unlikely to be the case. There's also a Malaysian woman in the database who is probably a distant relative. In the future, when the statistical analyses have improved and there is more DNA in the database, the results will be much more precise. I can imagine that not everyone will feel comfortable about this kind of test, but for me it has absolutely been worth the time and money.

DNA testing techniques are developing very rapidly at this time. In the near future, it will certainly become an accessible and reliable method for discovering more about your roots or about other family members. It is, however, good to realise that at the moment there is still considerable uncertainty about the significance of the test results. According to Jeroen, you also need to be open for a bit of pioneering and finding things out for yourself.

If you would prefer not to pioneer and do detective work, you can also have your DNA recorded in a professional databank. You get the most reliable results from experienced, certified organisations.

MAKING CONTACT

Meeting your family can be helpful in the process of mourning. But that's certainly not the only possible way of making contact. A visit to your foster parents, guardians or former carers can also have a healing effect. San Ho (42) from South Korea says:[41]

> It was the female director of the orphanage who, after a long conversation, threw her arms around me. I can't describe how warm that hug felt, however stupid that may sound. I'd been looking for that feeling of security all those years. Even though I didn't find my birth mother, that day I did find a place of rest in my life.

You can also make contact or connect by visiting your birth country. Rien (43) achieved some recognition by eating the food in the land of his birth, South Korea:[42]

The real home-coming consisted of something quite different for me. I worked in the restaurant business and love good food. I was and always will be very discriminating about food, about what tastes good and what doesn't. In Korea, eating together is important. I was given all kinds of food to eat. I ate all of it and it was just what it should have been. Just what my taste buds wanted. Just what food is supposed to be. It all just made sense. That was the feeling of home-coming to me. Everything fell into place. This was the food that I ate for the first years of my life and the taste buds apparently remember that.

If you're adopted, you might feel pressure from the outside world to make contact with your birth family or birth country, while you yourself don't (yet) have any need for it. If that's the case, it's important to keep listening to your own feelings and not let yourself be influenced by the opinions of others. Anneke Vinke discusses this in an interview:[43]

There are adoptees who say: 'I'm never going back.' Fine. Nothing wrong with that. There are also adoptees who from the age of five want nothing more than to go back. Also fine. If you look at the figures from the research carried out by Wendy Tieman,[44] you can say that, very generally speaking, a third of all adopted children want to search for their birth family. Then there's another third who especially want to get more information and a third who don't feel any need to search. If you look at programmes like *Spoorloos*,[45] you get the idea that all adoptees want to go back. That puts pressure on adoptees, because they don't have the chance to choose their own way. People very often are asked: 'Oh, you're adopted; have you been back, then?' That puts on a kind of pressure.

RESEARCHING YOUR FAMILY HISTORY

Often you can more easily accept things if you find out more about the actual living situation of your parents and ancestors. The 'systemic work' is based on this and can help with it.

If you can reconstruct the family history of your birth parents (something which is unfortunately impossible for many adopted children), you can draw a *'genogram'*; this is a kind of family tree in which you make your family history visible. In a genogram, you place all of your family members up to and including your grandparents. Often it then becomes clear, for example, who died prematurely, who was divorced, and so on. It can help you to gain more insight into the behaviour of your birth and adoptive parents and into your position within all of these different family systems.

Ethiopian Felekesh (47), who took part in a discussion group of adoptees, says:[46]

> On the basis of letters which I had received from my African family, my genogram was also drawn. It had to do with my birth family, my adoptive family and the foster family. What everybody [in the group] agreed about was that it is very complicated for a child to find your place in all of those families. It was also good for me to put all of those families next to each other. Drawing a genogram is a very powerful instrument to see what your relationship is to everyone and everything, and where you come from.

Sometimes a conversation with one of your parents or another family member can shed new light on the history of your family. Former foster child Nicole (43) says:

> My younger sister died in a train accident when she was 14. She had been to the disco and had had too much to drink; she thought that she could still go between the barriers and cross the tracks. I was 17 at the time. My sister and I had been living at home again for a year. First I was in shock more than anything, and then I became sad, but as time passed I became more and more angry with my mother. She had given my sister too much freedom. She shouldn't have been standing at the railway crossing at midnight, she was only 14! For a long time I was very angry. It was only when I was 30 that I had a talk with my mother and she told me about her brother. He had committed suicide when he was 25 to escape from the stifling attention of my grandmother. My grandmother was extremely controlling. Her children couldn't do anything unless she knew all about it. My mother had decided that she would allow her children more freedom, so that that wouldn't happen. My mother looked so sad when she told me that. Suddenly I understood why it had

happened and my anger disappeared instantly. I hugged her and we cried together about the loss of her brother, my sister and her child.

PARTICIPATING IN A FAMILY CONSTELLATION

If you want to know more about your own feelings or if you have absolutely no information about your birth family, then a *'family constellation'* can also help you to make your position with respect to your own family more visible. You make, as it were, a 'family photo' or 'family film' in which you are an active participant. The 'family photo' is something that you make with someone who is specialised in *Systemic Constellation Work*. You put together your family with puppets or real people; it's an inner representation of how you perceive your family or families, how they are positioned or move with respect to each other. Some family members appear standing close to you and others further away, or, for example, with their back to you. In this family constellation you also include family members who have passed away. Your inward 'family image' can help you to experience in a more conscious way how, according to you, the energy in your family flows and what you need to make the energy flow more gently. During a family constellation sometimes you realise that things have to be discussed or said, and this gives you an opportunity to do that. Adoptees and foster children usually make a constellation in which both families appear. You can then discover what position you take in the two systems of foster/adoptive family and birth family, and what you might be able to change about that. Some people have no affinity at all for such a family constellation, but for others it provides genuine insight. Adoptee Sety Ditters writes this in a blog about a family constellation that she did:[47]

> I had the opportunity, unexpectedly, to take part in a family constellation workshop, in which I could introduce my own theme. During the workshop you get, in a very special, loving way, more insight into your situation and you can take a step forward in your

personal development. [...] It is difficult to explain what exactly happens, so you'll only understand it if you experience it yourself. But it isn't something vague; it's quite down to earth.

My theme was 'the dynamic and my place within my birth and adoptive family'. Before this family constellation I never dared to feel unprocessed emotions from the past; I've always let gratitude and positivity set the tone.

[...] During the workshop, everything that I already knew deep inside was confirmed and I was able to thank my late father that he'd given me a second chance. Apparently I needed the courage to step outside my comfort zone so that I could sincerely say farewell, and that's what I did. And it feels incredibly good!

Former foster child Marilyn (53) tells about her experience with a family constellation:

After the death of my mother, my father 'had' very many new women. My father was then always regarded as a 'womaniser'. I also thought so for years. One day I did a family constellation and I was asked: 'Was he looking for a new wife, or was he looking for a new mother for you?' I suddenly remembered his personal ads in the local church paper: 'Quiet widower seeks new mother for his children.' I also remembered again that when we were introduced to a new woman, he would say something like: 'This is Corrie, your new mother. I think that she would really like it if you called her Mum.'

Although I think my father was entirely disconnected from any of the real needs of his children, my opinion about his behaviour has changed since this family constellation. He isn't a womaniser to me any more. All those women were his clumsy attempts to take care of us.

If you want to know more about systemic work and family constellations, you can find appropriate books in the Further Reading list.

WRITING YOUR LIFE STORY

By writing your life story, you connect with your past at various levels. Important memories and experiences are given a place and gradually you discover a central theme. It gives you a deeper insight into yourself, your origins and your direction. Present, past and future become visible and connected with each other 'outside of yourself'. By putting it in words, you get a grip on and give structure to the story that in all sorts of ways invisibly tunnels inside you. You can acknowledge difficult events and losses and you might discover new lifegoals as a result. Willemieke (26), adopted from Indonesia, has this to say:[48]

> Writing this story is, to me, another step in the process of mourning. I think that in doing so I will give myself the possibility of processing the past, giving words to it, giving meaning to it and then learning how to deal with it. All of this in order to make it easier to express and understand my feelings in the future; in order to make me feel more confident in all kinds of situations where dealing with people is at the centre.

Children and adolescents can also benefit greatly from writing a life story in which their losses are made visible. They could make a 'life book' in which the story of their origin becomes visible. By beginning with their birth or even with their conception, carers can make all important periods visible. Both birth parents and foster or adoptive parents can be given a place in a life book. Everything that has happened (the good events and the not so good ones) can be identified. Even if little is known about a period, attention can be given to it.

Writing down your life story is a way of getting your story 'in order', little by little. In the Further Reading section I have listed various practical books which might be helpful with writing. Many writing courses can also be found on the internet via search terms such as '(auto)biographical writing' or 'writing life stories'.

KEEPING MEMORIES ALIVE

Connecting with your past through memories is important, but not always easy. Good memories can cause considerable pain, because they confront you with the fact that someone or something that you loved very much isn't there any more.

If you have negative or traumatic memories, it is even more complicated. On the one hand, it is important that you also dare to look at the unpleasant memories; processing the pain about these events can have a healing effect. On the other hand, it can also be healing to recall good memories. However small they are, they can help you to look at someone or something with more nuance and to experience new, positive feelings that you might have forgotten.

Former foster child Jenny (35), who was abused by her father for years, tells:

> I suddenly remembered last month how my father and I once walked past a music shop and that I saw a recorder lying in the window. I wanted to have it very much. My father said that the shop was closed, but I pointed to the open door and said that it was open. We went inside and in the end I got a real professional wooden recorder. It's very strange. I had forgotten that memory. He treated me so badly that nothing positive ever came to mind. I am very happy with this 'new' memory. I suddenly know now that he wasn't only bad, but that in his own way he also loved me.

Below, you'll find a few ideas about how you can recover unknown or forgotten memories and make them visible.

- Write one or more letters to the one you have lost. In this letter, call up some memories about them or write what you would still like to say to someone if he or she was still there.

- If your memories are vague, go and sit down in a comfortable chair, concentrate on the person you have lost and write down words that you associate with him or her. Don't make any distinction between positive and negative words. Sometimes it works better if you write with your left hand if you are right-handed; your non-dominant hand is directed more by your intuition, while your dominant hand is directed above all by your mind. Allow yourself some time, or write every day for a while. Choose words from the list that you want to write about and try to make short stories or poems with them. Keep them in a special box or folder.

- If your memories are limited – for example, predominantly negative – write them down or use a tape recorder. Read or listen to them a few days later. Is the memory still the same, or do you look at it differently now?

- Take advantage of other people's perspective: who else has memories of what or whom you have lost? Other people can offer extra dimensions to what you have lost. Are there friends or family members perhaps who look at it differently from you? Can they tell you anything nice about your parents from when they were still young, or about the time when your mother was pregnant? Do they remember, perhaps, something touching about the day of your birth?

The present: saying farewell and giving meaning

In order to connect with the present, it is important that you close out the past in a symbolic way. You can do this with a *farewell ritual*. Afterwards there is often room to live more in the present. In a farewell ritual, one of four elements – water, earth, fire, air – is frequently used. If someone dies, you say farewell by cremating someone (fire) or by burying him (earth). The ritual means that you mark something as past, and that you are aware that, from this day on, things will be different. The funeral or cremation can be an important memory of the life of someone who was dear to you. You might still have the speeches, the letters and cards, the photos that you can still look at. By looking at these, you form a new bond with the one who has died. And it also tells you that the life of the other person is truly over.

With a ritual you mark the past, so you can go forward into your future. Important milestones deserve clear markings. If that doesn't happen at the moment itself, then you can still do it at a later moment in your life.

For many foster children and adoptees, 'saying farewell to what has happened' is complicated, particularly because there is no clear beginning or end to the situation. Often there is still hope of renewed or improved contact with the first parents. Only when your father or mother dies is there a clearly marked moment. But, even then, it can be complicated to say farewell. It may still be helpful to think of a farewell ritual, so that you can move forward into the present.

You can go about a farewell ritual in three steps:

1. GIVE THE PAIN A SYMBOLIC FORM

By giving pain a symbolic form, you make your loss visible. This can help you in the grieving process. At the same time, you go forward in creating a new relationship with whom or what you have lost. Some people find the cross an appropriate symbol for the pain that they carry with them. Others think of a knife, a photo of yourself in a cracked mirror or a photo of the other person in a broken photo frame, a broken piece of glass. Perhaps you'll want to give your pain symbolic form by writing a story about it or by making a painting, a drawing or carving a sculpture. It can also be done by creating a dance or a special song, piece of music or poem. Another way to give form to your pain is by writing a farewell letter. In that way you address your grief and it won't continue to circulate within you. You could begin, for example, with the sentence 'If you were still here...' or 'If you were here now...'

2. THINK UP A FAREWELL RITUAL

If you have lived through your loss once more and have made it visible, you might want to consider a ritual farewell ceremony. You can do that, for example, by asking yourself:

- Which events/characteristics do I want to say farewell to because they are holding me back?

- What have I learned from the events that have been blocking me?

- Which events/characteristics do I want to take with me into the future because they are giving me support?

- What have I learned from the events that give me support?

- Which of the four elements (water, air, fire, earth) will I use for this ritual?

'Saying farewell' doesn't necessarily mean that you let something float away (water, air), cover it (earth) or burn it; it can also mean that you keep it with you and give it a visible place – for example, in your house, on your body or in nature. It depends on your own feelings. Some people love fire, because it has a fast, purifying power. Others experience it as 'destructive'. Former foster child Hanna (44) writes:

> I was once asked to throw a carefully written letter to my father in the fire as a way of saying farewell. But everything in me resisted doing that. In the letter, I had put all my feelings for him. In fact, I had my father back! I didn't throw the letter into the fire, but instead keep it in a beautiful box at home. Through the letter, I formed a new bond with him. It made me whole.

Ask yourself how you want to say farewell. You can transform something that was weighing you down into something pure. Maybe you will want to carry it with you for a while, until you don't need to any more, until you can store it away, bury or burn it. Or maybe you will want to keep the new object in your life forever, so that it's always close at hand. It's all about marking your loss, and about giving it a designated place in one way or another.

If you want to carry out a farewell ritual, you can consider whether you want to do it alone, or want to have friends or family with you. What clothes will you wear? What do you want to look like on that day or on that moment? You might want to take pictures or make a film of the ritual, or you might want your best friend or partner to say something.

3. BRING THE RITUAL TO A CONCLUSION AND DIRECT YOURSELF TO THE FUTURE

Bringing a ritual to a close and directing yourself to the future can have a healing effect. What will you take with you to the future? What space will you give this? You can also bring a ritual to a conclusion by diving into the sea, by taking a ritual shower, washing your hands, putting on new clothes and throwing the old ones out, having a nice meal with friends, organising a party, taking a trip, meditating. It is important that, by concluding this ritual, you establish a new connection with your past and your future. Ask yourself: how has this ritual affected me? Maybe there's someone with whom you can share this feeling. Take time for this final step. Bratawati (21), adopted from Indonesia, says:

> In Indonesia, I shovelled native soil from the spot where I was found. When I was back in the Netherlands, I bought a pendant that could be worn as a necklace. It was a pendant in the shape of a bottle, and you could open it. I put some native soil in it and my boyfriend hung it around my neck. Now I carry the earth of my native country visibly around my neck and that feels good. Since then, I understand the word 'to ground' much better, because that is precisely what that chain does with me: I feel connected with my place of birth.

Former foster child Marilyn (53) says this about saying farewell to her father, who was traumatised by war, and who often abused her:

> When my father died, I took the radio and his military uniform home with me. One evening, I put his clothing on, and his hat, and his shoes. In my view, my father was always a tall man, but I now came to realise that that wasn't the case at all. He was actually quite a short man. I hardly know my father except in his military uniform. It was a special revelation to wear his clothing and to see in the mirror how much I actually looked like him.

Later that evening I made a fire outside and I burned his clothing and associated things. That was very good. I still have his radio in my house, with some photos from before.

GIVING MEANING

If you manage to give meaning to a loss, you are much more likely to be able to direct yourself towards the future again. Questions you might ask yourself are:

- 'What could I do to give meaning to what has happened to me, so that I can go forward in life with a new sense of balance?'

- 'How can I pass on to others what I have learned from this loss?'

Giving meaning doesn't have to mean that you get 'answers'; it can also mean that you learn to go forward in life without being able or willing to attach meaning to your loss.

The Future: connecting with your own life once more

In order to go forward in your life, it is important that you grieve about what you have experienced. In the end, you'll then be able to reach a degree of acceptance concerning what has happened to you. If you don't seem to be able to reach some acceptance about what has happened – for example, because you've experienced too much – then Acceptance and Commitment Theory (ACT) might be able to help you. This verb 'to act' is precisely what this theory is about, specifically 'doing something'. ACT is at odds with many therapeutic and psychological models. It takes the position that you can get on with your life *without fighting the symptoms that are troubling you.* Harris (2012) gives a very simple description of what ACT is in a nutshell:[49]

- A = Accept: accept your thoughts and feelings and be present.

- C = Choose: choose a direction in life determined by values.

- T = Take action.

The point with this theory is that you create a meaningful life while you accept the pain that goes with it. At connecting theme three (making a connection with your heart), you could already read how, with the help of mindfulness and breathing exercises, you can make space for the pain. By that means, it will be easier to reach a state of acceptance from where you can begin to experience more peace.

Once you are in a position where you can accept your thoughts and feelings, you can, according to the theory of ACT, subsequently *act in the spirit of what you truly want*: you act on the basis of your values. Values are the things in life that matter to you personally. They have often been passed on to us in our upbringing and from the culture in which we've grown up. Nevertheless, people from the same family or the same culture don't necessarily have the same values. You choose (unconsciously) the values that are appropriate to your personality. Probably without you being aware of it, they guide your behaviour and your choices. They determine how you spend your time, and how you will respond to various life events. In reality, values are the innermost desires of your heart about how you want to behave as a person. They aren't goals, because you achieve goals and then cross them off your list. Values stay with you your whole life. They tell you how you want to *behave* (which is different from what you want to *achieve*). You can discover them by answering the following questions:

- What do I want to stand for in my life?

- Who do I really want to be?

- What kinds of behaviour really matter to me?

In the appendix at the back of the book, you will find a list of values. If you know your values, you can bring your life into conformity with them; what has happened to you will not then determine what path you take in life. Whatever path you follow in life will be the right one, provided you:

- can make room for what has happened
- can be gentle, accepting and attentive with respect to yourself and the world
- can live in accordance with your most important values.

Adoptee Liesbeth List (72), who, despite everything that happened to her, came to acceptance, tells how powerfully you can be driven by your values. Values like love, forgiveness, wisdom, optimism and empathy help her in that respect:[50]

> My parents did what they had to do. Giving up a child must be horrible. The poor wretches, who have no food and have to give up their children because they are unable to live, or because they are the victims of a war; that suffering is unimaginable. If you are adopted, that means that you were allowed to go on living. That's what counts.

> Forget the negative things. There's no point in fighting them or feeling bad about them. You can't change anything about the fact that you're an orphan or a child who grew up with complete strangers. Sometimes it works out well, sometimes it doesn't. […] But don't let the suffering pollute your mind and your heart. It's a miracle that you're still there. Love your life.

In the Further Reading list at the back of the book, I have included various titles about Acceptance and Commitment Theory. Most books are practical and have lots of exercises that you can do at home.

Questions
Knowledge questions

1. The Circle of Connecting has no beginning and no end. Why is that so important in the process of mourning?

2. 'The body' is in the middle of the illustration of the Circle of Connecting. What is the reason for that?

3. In adoptees and foster children, the stress regulation of the nervous system is often more sensitively set. In the Circle, various stress reducing techniques that can help in mourning are discussed. Name four. Why do these techniques reduce stress?

4. What are negative, automatic thoughts and beliefs? Explain how they can disturb mourning or the process of searching.

5. Connecting with your heart (*Theme 3*) is often especially difficult for adoptees and foster children. Why? When is it important to seek help in this regard?

6. In a process of mourning, it is important that you have the support of friends, family and those with similar experiences. Why is support so important? Name three functions that support can have.

7. Finding new information in your life story can result in a more nuanced image of reality. Think of an example of this.

8. By 'gathering information about your past' and 'making contact', people often think especially about locating relatives. What can a search produce besides this? Can you think of three examples of a search that could be very meaningful without relatives being located?

9. If you say farewell, you should also consciously take memories, facts and events with you to the future. What memories, facts or events might those be, for example?

10. If you mourn what has happened to you, ultimately you can often come to a greater acceptance. Sometimes a person has experienced so much that it isn't possible to grieve about everything. What methods can help you to achieve a greater measure of acceptance nevertheless?

11. Values can help you to direct your life to the future, despite everything that you have experienced. What are values? How can they help you?

Personal questions

1. Do you know people who have managed to live in conformity with their innermost values? Think of three examples.

2. Find in the appendix at least ten values that are important to you. Then choose the four or five most important ones. Which ones are they? What could you do to be able to live in conformity with these values?

CHAPTER 4

Contact with Your Birth Family

Mourning what is (not)

Foster children and adoptees come into contact with their birth families in many different ways. For both, the pain they feel because of the distance or because of what has happened plays an important role. Consequently, contact with the birth parents is seldom something that can be taken for granted. You probably ask yourself frequently how you relate to each other in different phases of your life.

If you were placed in long-term foster care, it is very likely that you had occasional contact with one or both of your birth parents during your childhood. Contact with your first parent(s) has then been a theme that has run through your life from your early years. Gina (26), a former foster child, tells about her contact with her birth father:

> Contact is difficult. The first time that I saw him, I was still young. I was afraid of him back then. The following times, I was an adult. The second and third times were a mix of fear, frustration, recognition, happiness, confusion, anger and loss. The last time, my partner and children were there too. That meeting was special. That time I felt, more than anything else, powerful and at peace.

Foster children who look back on their youth, often remember meetings which were associated with strong feelings of sadness, disappointment or anger. Jeremy (21), a foster child, tells this about such a meeting:

> I had been living in a foster family since I was three years old. I was happy there, felt acknowledged and at ease. I remember that we occasionally had an appointment at the Youth Care Office. I saw my mother there. I always looked forward to it, but it often happened that she didn't show up. Then I sat there waiting for her with my foster mother. The pain that I felt then is difficult to describe. I felt rejected and shut out. My mother had a new family, but there was no room for me. And she was always unpleasant to my foster mother. I had the feeling that I wasn't really allowed to love her. Very complicated.

If you're adopted, renewed personal contact with your birth parents is usually only possible when you're an adult. If you were adopted overseas, a meeting often only takes place after a successful search. When you meet your birth parents, that usually involves a lot of emotions. Suddenly, you're standing eye-to-eye with a blood relative: many adoptees experience an intense feeling of kinship at that moment. That first meeting usually marks the beginning of a new, life-long bond. That bond can produce great joy and recognition, but it can also summon up, for example, anger, guilt or fear. Angelo (21), who met his family at the age of 18, writes about the influence his search had on him:[51]

> My return to the country of my birth changed me irreversibly. I gained a family. That's wonderful, but it's also a cause of anxiety, because a day doesn't pass without me thinking about them or worrying whether they're OK. Processing my roots-journey was extremely heavy at times but it was worth it. The depression that lasted six months was very bad, but it was nothing by comparison with the fine things that I also got.

It's true for almost all adoptees and foster children that a relationship with the birth parents cannot be taken for granted.

A relationship based on trust can grow step by step, but it can also happen that such a relationship never develops or that it is gradually destroyed again. Frédérique (51), an adoptee, has this to say about her contact with her birth mother:

> I got to know my birth mother when I was 25. At first, I felt real recognition and happiness, but gradually the contact became more complicated. When my dear adoptive mother passed away, my birth mother was utterly unable to deal with it. She dropped me like a brick. Very complicated. I was very sad about the death of my adoptive mother, but my birth mother couldn't support me. We've talked about it often, but I don't think we'll ever put it behind us. We're still in touch, but we think too differently about fundamental things in life. Sometimes that hurts, but I can't do anything but accept that that's the way it is. I can't change her.

Adoptees as well as foster children frequently mourn this life-long bond. For most people, it is a life-long process of alternately connecting and letting go. There's a good chance that in that process you'll experience new or old feelings of loss again and again. They might be feelings of powerlessness, for example, or feelings of anger, sadness, guilt or shame. You might also feel insecure and frequently wonder whether the bond will be broken once again. This can lead to fear but also to a strong sense of responsibility to keep the bond intact. Frédérique (51) says this:

> My birth mother is in fact an impossible person. I can hardly agree with her about anything. But I don't mind that. I've gotten so much in my life and she's lost so much. I really wanted to break off all contact with her after our fight last year, but I don't think I can do that to her, make her lose her child a second time. I continue to believe that she's not aware of any wrongdoing, despite the long and clear conversations that we've had about it.

Contact during childhood

Many adopted and foster children already mourn in their childhood the contact that they do or do not have. During moments of contact with their parents, foster children are often confronted with their own feelings of loss as well as those of their parents. Some adopted children mourn, from their early years on, the broken and resumed contact with their parents, if, for example, the adoptive parents have been able to establish personal contact with the birth parents during childhood.

Since children in long-term foster care generally have a very different kind of contact with their birth parents during their youth, I make an explicit distinction between foster children and adoptees in the following section.

Foster children

For children in long-term foster care, contact with their birth parents during their childhood is often a source of stress and sadness. Feelings of loss which they might experience are:

- disappointment, pain about not being acknowledged or about being isolated

- pain about repeatedly being rejected

- fear about being abandoned again

- pain about insecurity / about the lack of a stable parent

- pain about missing their family and their familiar environment

- fear / trauma as a result of violence or abuse.

If your parents suffered from addiction or a psychiatric disorder, you were probably confronted with unpredictable behaviour by your parents often. They might not have appeared for appointments or they might have let you down completely. As a result of all the uncertainty, the lack of response or failure to appear for an appointment or the dispute for custody in court, contact might have broken down. The foster father of Liška (12) has this to say:

> The birth mother's visits have been a drama for four years now. We see her more often in the courtroom than during visits to Liška. It's unimaginable. Something has to change. We've come up

with all kinds of proposals, but the mother keeps coming up with new conditions. She has a history in psychiatry; many visits end in a drama: every month there's an appointment, but the mother often fails to show up, she doesn't even call to cancel. During the visits that do take place, mother and daughter are remote. Liška has often been disappointed by her mother. For Mother's Day and Christmas, Liška crafts elaborate cards, but she gets nothing in return. Liška's happy with just a birthday card that arrives five days late. But it's the one card in three years… All those things hurt us incredibly too. You're so powerless. I want Liška to have a bond with her parents so much, so that she can feel acknowledged and can share things with her parents; I know that in order to get some peace of mind in her life she needs to be able to get on well with her mother.

You might have experienced lots of turbulence and pain in the contact that you had with your parents in your early years. A foster mother writes about her 18-month-old foster daughter:

After a visit to her mother, she's often very upset. Her parents are usually very angry and frustrated and cannot calm down when they see their daughter; it only feeds their anger, it seems. And it's rare for that not to have its consequences. Our foster daughter picks up on the tension without fail. Sometimes she's restless for days afterwards. She keeps tossing and turning and she's constantly in tears.

You might be, as a child, overwhelmed by your parents with presents or candy during a visit. That can also have caused you to become confused. How are you supposed to relate to your parents? Adult foster children often remember the large presents very clearly. Former foster child Alice (47), for example:

When I met my father, he would always give me money. Once he even gave me a 50-pound note. It always felt stupid, as if he could buy our relationship in that way. The more he gave me, the less chance there was for ordinary contact. That's what it felt like to me. It was all about guilt and our inability to connect with each other. Very painful.

If your parents were prone to violence, you were probably afraid of meeting them. Alexander (25), former foster child, says:

> I was seriously abused by my mother. I never knew my father. I remember that my mother often came for a visit. The judge in juvenile court had ordered it. She was more or less rewarded by the judge with a visit to me if she behaved herself otherwise. I was always very nervous about meeting my mother. I had nightmares about it for days before it happened. Despite the fact that my foster parents prepared me carefully for the visits, it was often tense. And for days afterwards, I was completely out of sorts. I found it difficult to deal with that confrontation again and again.

A visit might also dredge up old memories, which might have made you anxious. Former foster child Emma (25) says:

> My parents loved each other, but they had a very violent relationship. I often witnessed their intense fights. That obviously had a powerful impact on me, even if I was too young to understand what was happening. When I was five, the Youth Care Office intervened. In the end, I was placed with my grandmother. She raised me from then on. It was only then that I learned what a 'normal' life was like and that adults could also be nice to each other. When my parents came for a visit at my grandmother's, they often still had fights. My grandmother tried to suppress that, but without much effect. They said very nasty things to each other. I was often upset for days after one of those visits; they gave me such an awful feeling. It was as if the whole world was going to be ruined.

There's a good chance that you continued living in fear of being abandoned or rejected by your parents again. Many foster children behave in socially desirable ways for that reason. Borys (34), a former foster child, says this about his childhood:

> I always had mixed feelings if I went to my mother's for a visit. On the one hand, I really wanted to see her; on the other, I felt insecure and tense because I never knew what we'd do. I was often left to sort myself out. When I returned from such a visit, I was often angry and disappointed because it hadn't been fun. I blamed

myself for that, although I was also angry with my mother because she hadn't made things pleasant. I found it difficult to define my boundaries with her; I was always afraid of hurting her. More than anything else I wanted to make her happy.

Former foster child Yuri was always afraid of being rejected during his childhood:

> I never dared to be unkind to my father. I was afraid that if we had an argument, I wouldn't be welcome any more. I often had the feeling that other things were more important to my parents than I was and so I felt rejected and insignificant. It was the same in my foster family and at school: I was always afraid of being sent away if I didn't try to be good.

Your foster parents might also have found it difficult to deal with your birth parents, or vice versa. That might also have been a source of stress or sadness. A child has a fundamental need to have permission from both parties for the new situation. Only then can he or she experience peace of mind. Evette (35), a former foster child, says this about her foster parents:

> My foster parents had a deep dislike of my mother. They wouldn't show this openly but I could always tell. If I'd been to her for a visit, they were always overprotective. They asked me if I'd had a good time. I once heard my foster mother say to a foster care worker that my mother lived in a dirty house and that she couldn't even look after herself. That hurt me. I didn't think that her house was dirty at all. It was always really nice to be at my mother's house. But somehow they had an influence on me. I didn't feel like I could be genuinely happy when my mother came for a visit. When I was 15, my mother passed away. We didn't talk much about that either. I hid the sadness that I felt at the time from my foster parents. I was never really allowed to bond with her and I resent them for that. I never actually dared to connect with her and that's something that I still experience as a great loss in my life.

Sandra, a foster mother, tells about the peace of mind that you can gain if parents give each other 'permission for contact':

> The contact with Sandy's birth mother is more peaceful than it used to be. Sandy also reacts more calmly now after she's been for a visit. Especially since her mother gave Sandy a kind of 'permission' to live with us and verbalised this to Sandy. Before that, Sandy reacted very intensely to the visiting arrangements.

Most foster children have a deep-rooted sense of loyalty to their birth parents. There's a good chance that deep in your heart you have a desire to 'go home to where you belong', however pleasant it is in your foster family. That desire is a source of great sadness to many foster children, even if they no longer expect anything from their birth family. Bernice (25) explains:

> I was 13 when I was placed with a foster family. I had been abused and mistreated by both of my parents. Fortunately, I found myself in a kind foster family, where I could catch my breath. But after six months things began to gnaw at me. However nice and safe it was with my foster family, I missed my parents. When I told my foster mother that, she was stunned. There was a kind of outrage in the way she looked at me. 'How could I want that?' I could see her thinking. My parents were bad, weren't they? How could I possibly miss them? I never dared to say that to anyone again. But when I was lying in bed at night, I often cried, I wanted to be with my own parents so much and go to sleep in my own bed. To be honest, I've never gotten over that sadness, even now that I'm an adult.

You might also wonder if you're allowed to love your foster parents. Gulsah (28), a foster mother, who's raising the children of her deceased sister, tells about her foster son Cagatay (8):[52]

> He will show his feelings unexpectedly. I remember one time when I was busy getting ready for Eid al-Fitr that he suddenly said: 'Gulsah, I do still miss my mother. I can't get her out of my head.' I was sobbing and I explained to him that he didn't have to get her out of his head at all. A while later he said: 'I love you too, you know.'
>
> When we were sitting next to each other on the bus once he said to me: 'Now it seems just like you're my Mum.' I told him that I

was honoured to hear him say that, but that no one could take the place of his mother. Sometimes I think he's fighting within himself. He wants to accept me as a mother but he feels guilty about it too.

Adopted children

Adopted children only gain the right to access their birth records when they turn 18. From that moment they can also establish personal contact with their birth parents, if their identity is known. Some adoptees, however, have already had contact with (one or both of) their birth parents from an early age; that might be the case if you have been adopted into a new family via an 'open adoption'. If, for example, you've been adopted from the United States, you probably know the names of your birth parents; in many cases, they will have chosen your adoptive parents themselves. You might, then, have had occasional contact with your birth parents as a child. It might also be the case that you had contact through letters or that your adoptive parents successfully searched for your family during your youth and that you've met them one or more times.

Contact with your birth parents probably gave you peace of mind to some extent, but it probably also gave rise to dormant feelings of loss. Since you were still young when you got to know your birth parents, you might have found it especially difficult to deal with the emotions involved. Tim (19), adopted from the United States, had this to say:

> My adoptive parents have had contact with my birth family since I was born. I really liked that. I knew my entire family from my first years and, for that reason, I had many fewer questions about where I originally came from. Every year we went to America to visit my family. That was always very nice. But I also always had many, many questions and some things hurt me badly. For example, I come from a very large family, and I was the only one who was adopted. I found that difficult to understand, especially when I was still young. When we were leaving after a visit, my parents always took a picture of me with all my sisters and brothers and cousins.

On the one hand, that was really a nice memory, of course, but on the other hand it was also horrible to have to leave again. I belonged there with them, but I also belonged with my adoptive parents. It was very complicated for me as a child to deal with that.

When you met your birth parents or had to leave them again, they might have been intensely sad about having put you up for adoption and that might have been very difficult for you. Or your first parents might have turned out to be so poor that they can hardly provide for their most basic needs. That might have given you a deep sense of personal responsibility for their future happiness. Commonly occurring feelings of loss which adopted children can have from contact with their birth family include:

- fear of being rejected again
- sadness, anger or disappointment about the reasons for being put up for adoption
- sadness or a feeling of being pulled apart as a result of being put up for adoption/living in two worlds
- disappointment, the pain of not being acknowledged or of being isolated
- sadness about saying goodbye and missing your family.

Maybe your birth family lived overseas, which meant that you couldn't travel there easily. That might also have caused you sadness. Hanna (23), adopted from Senegal, says this:

When I was 11, I met my birth parents. That was intense, but also wonderful. I look a lot like my mother and my little sister and that immediately gave me self-confidence. I was very happy that I knew my family now. But it also gradually made me very sad. I felt like a child of two families, one from Senegal and one from the UK. I started missing my sisters and my parents in Senegal more and more, but I didn't want to lose my brother and my adoptive parents. That caused confusion and sadness. I often asked my parents if my family couldn't come here. I couldn't really understand why they couldn't.

Siline, adopted from Ethiopia, says:

> I got to know my birth parents when I was nine. My feeling of connectedness with my birth family was immediately strong. But it also gave me a feeling of powerlessness. Whenever anything happened in the area around Addis Ababa (where I was born), I became concerned. There were lots of phone calls back and forth, to find out if they were alright. When I was 13, my sister was going to be married and I really wanted to be there. But I wasn't allowed to miss school, which was very frustrating for me. I kept feeling the powerlessness of not being able to go there. When my sister suffered a miscarriage, once again we couldn't go there. The feeling of connectedness with my family is a very fine thing, but it also caused lots of sadness. It was difficult to deal with that as a child.

Siline also always found saying goodbye to his family very difficult:

> Meeting my family was always one huge party. It was wonderful to be together, something that you couldn't express in words. That made the heartbreaking farewell which inevitably followed all the more painful. After I'd left, my birth mother didn't sleep for a week. She was so sad, and she lost her appetite. And I felt just the same. I was always very upset when I got home and it took at least a week to recover.

Contact with your first family usually doesn't only release painful feelings. Positive, connecting feelings come into existence because you learn to know yourself better by knowing your birth family and/or because you find answers to complicated questions. You might be able to take some significant steps forward in the mourning process as a result.

> *You carry feelings of loss from your youth with you into adulthood. If you haven't mourned them yet, the Circle of Connecting might help you to get started. As I wrote in Chapter 2 (section 'Factors that hinder the mourning process' on p.66), there can be factors which make it complicated to mourn for the losses that you suffered in your youth relying only on your own resources.*

The first (renewed) contact during adulthood

If you haven't had contact with your birth parents for a long time or if you've never met them, the moment of (renewed) contact is a meaningful event. There's a good chance that you've been preparing for this moment for a very long time. What will it be like? Will I look like her? Will he accept me? Will I get answers to my questions? Will we get on?

In Chapter 4, I've described a number of steps you can take to prepare. You can:

- pay attention to your physical health (*Theme 1*)

- identify your expectations and consider how realistic and helpful they are (*Theme 2*)

- learn a good breathing technique and develop body awareness so that you can make room for your feelings (*Theme 3*)

- think about the people who might be able to give you some support and who you can involve in your preparations (*Theme 4*)

- connect with your past – for example, by learning the language of your parents or learning about the history, culture and customs and values of your parents (*Theme 5*)

- think about a ritual that you might like to carry out during or after the meeting (*Theme 6*)

- identify your own values, so that you know what you consider to be important in life (*Theme 7*).

Thorough preparation can be very valuable and helpful at the moment of meeting. Feiko (24), a former foster child, says:

> Via my grandmother, I'd established contact with my father. I hadn't seen him since I was seven. First, we connected via Facebook, which was very nice. I could already get used to him a bit at a distance. My father is an addict and just lives in a very different world from me. Through that contact on Facebook, I saw what

his life was like and what was important to him. I'd also seen a few pictures of him. When I finally met him, it was as if I already knew him a little. The really severe tension had been removed, which I was grateful for.

During the meeting, you should nurture:

- a good breathing technique and good physical condition (sleep well, get enough exercise to release the tension, eat healthy food) (*Theme 1*)

- acceptance of your feelings; make room for them and don't fight against them (*Theme 3*)

- sufficient support from family members and friends who you love (*Theme 4*).

Joanne (30), a former foster child who met her birth mother again when she was 29, tells how helpful it can be during a meeting to make room for your feelings:

> My birth mother lives in a psychiatric institution. I met her twice as a child, but these meetings were not a success. I was terribly afraid of her both times. I was dreading meeting her again. I kept putting it off. But last year I suffered a burn-out and my therapist convinced me to visit her again. She helped me to get ready step by step. She taught me, among other things, how to control my emotions better. I practised breathing techniques and learned that fighting against your feelings usually only makes things worse. I really benefited from that when I met my mother. I knew how to accept my feelings and at the same time remain relatively calm. It felt really good, my fear was gone and I could really make contact with her.

Common feelings of loss after the first contact

What your first contact will be like depends on many factors. The culture, the history and the circumstances have a significant influence. In any case, this important new relationship will set many things in motion from the moment when the meeting takes place. Below, I will discuss a number of frequently occurring feelings of loss which can play a role in the first phase of this new relationship.

CONFUSION

There's a good chance that you will be confused following the first (renewed) meeting. So much has happened; you've experienced so much. What, for example, is your place in the new family? Do you belong in it? Or has being placed in foster care or having been adopted made you into something of an outsider? You might not feel you are part of the family because your parents argue all the time or tell conflicting stories, which makes it difficult for you to fit in. You might also be confused because your birth family has very different expectations for the new relationship than you do. Adoptee Laura (27) feels confused because her birth parents put too much pressure on her:[53]

> I first met my birth mother. She responded [unemotionally], just like me. I quickly realised that she was mostly interested in the wealth that she thought I had. That really made me angry. I didn't want to feel responsible for her problems. She didn't help me either; she just gave me up. Later, my birth father appeared. It seemed that he hadn't seen my mother for a long time. He was very emotional and wanted to hug me the whole time. I'm not that physical and that put me off. But it also bothered me that he kept calling me 'his daughter'. I'm not his daughter. By calling me that, he was being unfair to my adoptive father. Since then, I've kept everyone at a distance.

You might be confused after the first meeting because you're not sure how your relationship should develop. Lavinia (30), adopted from South Korea, says:[54]

> I'm glad that I took the step of meeting my father. It enriched me and made me more mature. At the same time, I have lots of doubts about where to go from here. You've opened a Pandora's box after all; what do you do with the contents? People say that they gain peace of mind by doing that kind of thing, but it seems more like a

drug to me: it feels great at the moment, but later you feel slightly hung-over. My father and I met again a year after the first meeting and we have some email contact. For me that first meeting was actually enough, but you can't close the box again once it's been opened. You have to consider that carefully before you begin.

- Think ahead of time about the possible demanding or, by contrast, remote way that your birth parents might behave (*Theme 5*, making the wider context visible). How are you going to deal with their response? Consider that they probably have a very different perspective from you. Think carefully about that before the meeting. This way you will be better prepared. Often you'll then be less taken off guard by the unfamiliar, confusing feelings.

- Accept that after the meeting you might not have answers to a number of questions; give room to your confusion (*Theme 3*). You might need a time-out or only have contact via email or letters. Take the time to think things through carefully and let it sink in; it's normal not to know how to deal with everything. If you let enough time pass, the answers usually come.

- Be kind to yourself if you feel at first that you don't want any contact any more. Feelings can't be forced and you're not the only one who's felt that way. Sometimes that feeling turns out to be 'definitive' and you no longer try to make contact. Sometimes it turns out to be possible to build up a bond after all. Some people gradually discover that there are other members of the family that they do connect with and with whom they do want to maintain contact.

- Connect with your body, make sure that you get enough sleep and exercise, and eat healthy food. Make use of your breathing technique in order to feel more relaxed (*Theme 1*).

- Look for people in a similar situation or friends with whom you can talk about what you're going through (*Theme 4*).

- Ask yourself: Why didn't we connect? What differences are there between us? Is it because of cultural differences? Age differences? Different ways of communicating? The conditions that you've each placed on the relationship? The expectations that you each have? What might help? (*Themes 2 and 5*)

FEAR OF REJECTION

You might be afraid that your birth mother or father will once again reject you when the initial curiosity has been satisfied. That can make you feel insecure. Former foster child Kira (32) has this to say:

> My mother was always angry with me, she always gave me the idea that I did everything wrong, that I said the wrong things, that I wore the wrong clothes, and on and on. When I was a child, I always felt insecure with her. I was hoping that it would be different now; I'm grown up after all and I really wanted to be in contact again. But when I first saw her again last year, I felt insecure, just as I did years ago. That same old feeling rose up, as if it had never gone away. I was really afraid that she'd reject me again. She couldn't do that all over again, could she?

If you're afraid of being rejected, it is likely that you'll avoid contact. Or that you go ahead with the meeting, but get angry quickly when it doesn't go the way you want it to. You might be extremely sensitive to criticism then, so that a small comment or remark gives you the feeling right away that everything is wrong with you or with the other person.

- Ask yourself why you're so insecure. What ideas and assumptions is that based on? And are the assumptions realistic? What could you do to see to it that they don't have a hold over you any more? What thoughts could help you with that? (*Theme 2*)

- Take care that you have a good breathing technique and an awareness of your body, so that you head keeps communicating with your heart and you don't become overwhelmed with fear. (*Themes 1 and 3*)

- Ask yourself what values you consider to be most important. What does that say about you? Do those values change if you're rejected? (*Theme 7*)

GUILT

You might begin to feel guilty if, for example, you don't immediately feel an emotional connection with your birth family. Arjan (43) tells about his first meeting with his Greek mother:[55]

> I came back to the hotel after my first meeting and I was overwhelmed by all of the attention and love and wonderful things that I'd experienced. I felt almost guilty because I really couldn't feel anything for her at that moment. Of course, now I think that that's perfectly understandable, because if you haven't seen someone or known someone for 43 years, you can hardly expect to immediately love someone unconditionally.

You might also have to deal with feelings of guilt if things are going badly for your parents or family. You might now realise that you've always lived carefree and in comfort while your parents had to struggle or were sick or unhappy. Adoptee Laura (27) says:[56]

> My trip really calmed me down. When I had heard, over there, the story of my sister, who's two years younger than I am, I was confronted with the hard reality of the disaster that I had escaped and of how fortunate I really am. What she had to endure as a child could have been my life. For a long time that gave me a kind of guilty feeling. I can place that better now: children are the victims of the dealings of the parents. They are not to blame. What my sister had to experience, I couldn't do anything about. As a child, I also had to accept my fate.

Former foster child Hayden (35) felt guilty because he had never missed his mother:

> I hadn't seen my mother for 30 years. Really, I'd hardly missed her. I have great foster parents; to me, they're my 'real' parents.

> But last year I received a letter from my mother. She was very ill and wanted badly to meet me. When I was with her, she told me her complicated life story. Even though she'd never contacted me, she always missed me. Her sadness touched me deeply. Every year she had written a card for my birthday, but she'd never sent one. I looked at the pile of cards, 34 in total, one for each year. My heart broke. I'd never longed for my mother, but she had for me. I suddenly felt like a horribly selfish person. Now I take care of her every day. She doesn't have long to live. Maybe I can still make up for it a little.

Think carefully about feelings of guilt that you might have and be patient with yourself. What insights have you gained about yourself and what do you intend to do with them? Think about your own role in the story. What could you have done differently or did you want to do differently? Take some steps in the Circle of Connecting:

- Accept that you're sad about this; make room for the pain. (*Theme 3*)

- Look for support in your surroundings, talk with others about your feelings of guilt so that you can defuse them. (*Theme 4*)

- Search for memories and try to make them visible. (*Theme 5*)

- Think of a ritual to identify the pain, so that you can say farewell to it (*Theme 6*). Try to look for a way of making sense of it.

- Accept what has happened and choose your values. If you feel a need to, undertake concrete steps to change the situation. (*Theme 7*)

ANGER

During the meeting or soon after, you can discover things which cause you to be angry. You might find out that you have sisters and brothers who were allowed to grow up with your parents; your father and mother might not have been honest about the past or they might turn out to be rather unscrupulous. Angelo (21), from Columbia, met his birth parents and it left him with some very unpleasant feelings:[57]

> Anyone who is planning to take a roots-journey has to realise that he will never be the same person as he was before his roots-journey. Consider carefully that you might hear unpleasant things about your parents or that you might find yourself in some unpleasant situations. That they're constantly asking you for money, for example. Or that you find out that you have sisters and brothers who were able to grow up with your parents.

Felipe (20), an adoptee, met his Brazilian family when he was 18. They got on so well that it caused him problems afterwards:

> I met my family in Brazil. It was too good to be true. Everything was right. For two weeks I was with my mother, half-sister and grandfather, together with my adoptive parents. The rest of the large family was there now and then, and took us with them for day trips. I was the prodigal son and I had returned. It was very good. I just wanted to stay there. That's where I belong. That's what I saw and felt.
>
> When I was home again, I knew what I had to do. I got a job and saved for a ticket to Brazil. I wanted to go back, make up for lost time with my mother, learn the language. But as the months passed, I became depressed and angry. Why did my mother put me up for adoption? She had a family that I could easily have grown up in. I became so angry that I closed up. I could feel myself slowly getting more and more depressed. I think that I couldn't handle the intensity of the pain. I finally looked for help and found it, and I learned to verbalise about the pain that I felt. Then I was able to defuse my pain and that helped a lot.

Sometimes you become deeply disappointed because you realise after the meeting that your father or mother will never be (or be able to be) there for you. Former foster child Sandra (31) says:

> I wanted to meet my mother after the birth of my daughter. I had seen her for the last time when I was nine. I felt a strong need to show her my child. I was really looking forward to seeing her again, but I was setting myself up for a disappointment. She was hardly interested in my daughter. She only wanted to talk about herself and her problems. When she left, I felt incredibly angry. Why couldn't she listen to me just for once and show some interest in my child? I felt like breaking all the windows in her house, which of course I didn't do. It took months before I could control my anger.

It's important to take your anger seriously and to defuse it. Anger usually conceals sadness or disappointment. It's likely that deep within you have the need to be held, seen or 'acknowledged'. There might be someone in your surroundings who can satisfy your need to be, literally or figuratively, held, seen or 'acknowledged'. Consider the themes in the Circle of Connecting; which themes might help you during this period of your life? In order to give your anger some direction, you can, for example:

- Defuse the energy of your anger by getting lots of exercise. (*Theme 1*)

- Apply a good breathing technique and develop your body awareness, so that you don't drown in your anger. (*Themes 1 and 3*)

- Make room for your anger. (*Theme 3*)

- Share your feelings with others. (*Theme 4*)

- Try to make sense of your experience by means of a ritual. (*Theme 6*)

- Identify the values that are important to you. What have you learned from this situation? How can you make use of that in the future? (*Theme 7*)

SADNESS

You might discover that your mother or father has died and that you're too late to meet them. You can be overwhelmed, then, with intense sadness. Or your parents might still be alive, but you realise when you meet them just what you've missed all those years. Former foster child Jacky (42) grew up in various foster families and tells about her renewed contact with her mother:

> When we finally met each other after all those years, everything fell into place. I looked exactly like her – our voices, eyes, gestures were the same. We even laughed the same way. My mother told a very sad tale about my placement in foster care, but despite all of the sadness we really got on well together. I finally had a real mother too and she looked like me. I could have shouted for joy.
>
> When I was back in my own home, I was overcome with sadness. The lost years suddenly loomed up. It was unbearable to think about how it might have been if I could just have stayed with my mother. I'm sure that we would have been very happy together, but fate prevented it. It was just like someone pulled me down. I collapsed in a pool of unhappiness. We would never be able to get the years back again.

Sandra (37), a German–Turkish woman, experienced the sense of loss when she saw the pictures of her family for the first time:[58]

> I can see it. For the first time in my life, I see the people. I can see that they're my family. I can feel it. It's very intense. I feel it right down to the marrow in my bones. To see a picture of your father so late in life! And to suddenly feel what you've missed. I always thought that I had never missed him.

- Make room for your sadness, however difficult that might be (*Theme 3*); it has everything to do with the pain you feel for what could not be.

- Make sure that you have an effective breathing technique and develop more body awareness, so that you don't drown in sorrow. (*Theme 1 and 3*)

- Make sure that you have people around you who can give you support. (*Theme 4*)

- Search for memories and make them visible. (*Theme 5*)

- Think about a farewell ritual with which you can mark this period. (*Theme 6*)

- Accept what has happened, make sense of what has happened to you. What have you learned from it? What have you gained from it? How can you make use of that in the future? (*Theme 7*)

DEPRESSION

After the first meeting, you might have melancholy feelings. You might find that it's been less satisfying than you had hoped. Former foster child Inon (31), who became reacquainted with his mother when he was 24, says:

> When I met my mother, she seemed to be very kind and empathetic. I was so happy that we were finally in touch again. We immediately made another appointment, but the second meeting was a disappointment. She'd been drinking and she was very focused on herself. She told me that she had hardly any money and she was complaining about everything and everyone. She also made clear to me that she expected me to help her out; after all those years, I could give her something back, she thought. I went home with mixed feelings. We've made a couple more appointments since then, but I kept being disappointed. I found that difficult to accept. First, I was hoping for a renewed and good bond, and now I had to give up that hope.

The meeting might have been wonderful, but afterwards you don't really feel happy. Adoptee Danny (34) says:

> I really had a relapse after the meeting with my first father. That really surprised me. I'd been looking forward to the meeting for months. And suddenly my search was behind me. The mission was accomplished. I could look back with satisfaction, but I didn't. I had a really empty feeling. Nothing interested me any more. I wasn't interested in work and I didn't feel like discussing the meeting with others. Somehow nothing compared to the meeting that I had with my father. More than anything else I just wanted to lie in bed all day.

Curtains closed. Telephone off. Very strange. I had no idea how to get on with life.

- Connect with your body. Participate in a sport, eat healthy foods, and make sure that you get enough daylight. (*Theme 1*)

- Investigate your thoughts and assumptions. What expectations did you have for the meeting? Were they realistic? Say farewell to any unrealistic expectations and replace them with more realistic and helpful thoughts. (*Theme 2*)

- Make room for your depressed feelings (*Theme 3*). Give yourself time to catch your breath. Accept that at the moment you just don't know. A sense of direction in your life should naturally reassert itself, but it might take a while. If it takes too long, or proves unmanageable, seek the advice of a professional.

- Talk with others about your feelings and don't try to find a solution right away. (*Theme 4*)

Coping with rejection

If you are (once again) rejected by your birth parents, you might feel very alone in the world. You probably regret the day you embarked on your search, and you regret that you listened to those who encouraged you to undertake it. Who were those people who gave you that advice? You might have the feeling that your whole world has collapsed. How are you supposed to get on with your life? There's no way back and there doesn't seem to be any way forward. It's important that you find a path once again that will take you forward. Strategies from the Circle of Connecting might give you some help:[59]

PREPARE YOURSELF WELL
Before a meeting, consider your expectations carefully and be as realistic as possible about them (*Theme 2*). Before a meeting, you

should also carefully consider all of the possible scenarios. What if the other party doesn't respond at all? What if you are already rejected at the first meeting? What if your family doesn't want to have any more contact after the first meeting? If you don't feel ready to deal with these situations, then postpone the meeting.

EXPRESS YOUR ANGER

Make sure that you can express your anger and your pain. That might sound easy, but for many people it isn't. You're probably full of anger and disappointment; 'dealing with it constructively' is probably the last thing that you can or want to do. You might be inclined to take it out on someone. If you can't subdue the anger or the pain of rejection, or if you feel the need to hurt yourself or someone else, I strongly advise you to seek professional help.

Look for themes in the Circle of Connecting that might help you, for example *Themes 1, 3, 4* or *5*. Who are you so angry with? How can you express your anger in a constructive way? Write about it, take care to have an effective breathing technique, participate in a sport or take a walk, talk with people, try to direct your energy outside of you in a constructive way, however difficult that might be for you. Ask yourself: what need is concealed beneath my anger? How can I make sure that that need is (at least in part) satisfied?

TRY TO DETERMINE THE REASON FOR THE REJECTION

It might help if you try to determine the reason for the rejection (*Theme 5*, making the context visible). In many cases, the reason has nothing to do with you, and everything to do with the situation in which your birth family finds itself. A rejection can, for example, have the following reasons:

- The fact that she put you up for adoption has always been a great secret, which means that your mother can't allow you into her life. Her fear about it being revealed to people outside of her immediate surroundings is so great that she cannot (yet) make any room for contact with you.

- Your mother is trying to protect her new family and sees contact with you as a threat.

- The reason for putting you up for adoption is too painful and is associated with a traumatic, repressed memory – for example, of rape, violence or incest.

- Your parents are so ashamed that they were unable to care for you or feel so guilty about it that they have repressed what happened and (still) cannot face it.

- The memories of the circumstances surrounding your birth or adoption are too painful; your parents aren't up to dealing with them.

- Your parents have been so damaged by life psychologically that they don't have the skills to relate to you in a loving way.

- Your parents don't have the cognitive capacity to understand what has happened and cannot deal with your request.

- During the first renewed contact, you've told your parents that you are homo- or transsexual and in the culture of your birth parents that is completely unacceptable or even illegal.

- You have a disability and in the culture of your birth parents the disability means that you'll bring 'bad luck'.

Soon after a rejection, it's probably very difficult to accept this perspective on your birth parents. Take your own feelings seriously. There is usually only room and understanding for the other person's story once you've managed sufficiently to defuse your own feelings. Try to be kind to yourself. The rejection that you've suffered doesn't have anything to do with you; it has to do with the powerlessness of your parents. It might help to read stories about mothers who've given a child up for adoption or about people who've had the same experience as you. You can also find stories about other people's experiences on many websites. These resources might help you to understand your experience better and accept it.

LOOK FOR OTHER FAMILY MEMBERS OR PEOPLE ASSOCIATED WITH THE FAMILY

Sometimes there are other family members or people associated with the family who are receptive to contact (*Theme 5*, collecting information). These contacts can also be very valuable and healing. You'll often learn more about your family from them and eventually come to understand their rejection better.

MAKE SURE THAT YOU HAVE SUFFICIENT SUPPORT

Sometimes you can't process a rejection all on your own. Look for people in your immediate surroundings with whom you can share your story with (*Theme 4*). It might be a friend or relative or even someone outside of your family circle. You can look for someone who has gone through a similar experience or a professional counsellor that you get on well with. You can also share your story on special forums, where you can also read the stories of others. This is Cora's statement:[60]

> She sent a letter, my natural mother, saying that I wasn't her daughter as far as she was concerned, and please not to contact her. So I came in and talked to the intermediary quite a lot about that and I also started seeing a therapist for a bit as well... Angry, very very very angry... I wouldn't discourage anybody from trying, but I would ask to make sure that anyone who tries to trace [their birth family] is supported by a professional and by people who are outside of their adoptive family and outside their circle of friends.

In conclusion, it's important that you try to accept things, however difficult it might be, and try to give meaning to the rejection (*Themes 6* and *7*). How could this have happened? What can you learn from this for the future?

Making sense of your experience

If after the first (renewed) meeting you want to advance your personal development, it's important that you make sense of what you've experienced (*Theme 6*). You can make sense of it by:

- looking back on what you've experienced, and

- reflecting on your own behaviour, thoughts and emotions.

LOOKING BACK

'Looking back' means that you consider once again your life story and supplement it with the things that you've learned; in this way, there will be more themes connecting present, past and future. Writing down or telling your life story, for example, can have a healing effect and it can allow you to give closure to an important period of your life. Former foster child Jaeden (26) says:

> After 20 years, I located my father again. It's not possible to describe what that did to me. It was as if I was put back together as a new person. It was a beautiful and intense period.

> The most difficult thing for me after we had met was to get back to living my ordinary life. A huge gulf had opened up between the present and the past, and no one realised that that had happened to me. I had found my father and he was part of my life again. After a few weeks, I became depressed, even though the meeting had been a wonderful experience. In the end, I looked for help. I learned how to extend slender lines across that huge gulf. Stories, memories, I learned how to put the experience into words – the lines became cables, and in the end it became a bridge. I can walk across it now, to be in the past, but I can also return to the present. My father is part of the past, but also of the present and future. What it's all about is connecting everything with everything and making it visible. Extending the lines, that can be hard work, but in the end it really helps.

REFLECTING

By reflecting on what you've experienced, you can make sense of the meeting with (one of) your parents. 'Reflecting' means that you ask yourself questions that will teach you something about yourself. You take a look at your own behaviour, your thoughts, your patterns of response, the choices you make, how this makes you feel. In this way you increase your self-knowledge and you gain insight into your response patterns and into the feelings that you experience in certain situations. That makes it possible for you to change what you feel with respect to others and to the world.

Questions for reflecting include:

- What are the most important feelings I had during the meeting and afterwards?

- What, to me, is the most important thing that happened? What did I learn about myself as a result?

- Did I find out things that sparked deep emotions in me? What does that tell me about myself? What do I think about that? How will I deal with that?

- Did someone make a claim on me or disappoint me? How do I feel about that? What does that say about me? What does it say about the other person?

- What was my contribution to the occurrence of a certain situation?

- Do I recognise certain feelings and patterns of response in myself from earlier situations in my life? What does that say about me?

- If I could do it all again, what would I do differently? What does that say about me?

- Did the meeting change my values?

- How can I apply what I have learned to my life?

Continued contact in adulthood

If you are in contact with your birth parents during your adult life, another dynamic will develop. You'll build up a relationship which is more one of 'equality', but, as a result of your past, contact is not likely to become self-evident.

Feelings of loss

As a result of the contact with your birth parents, old feelings of loss can re-emerge. Earlier losses smoulder under the surface and a bit of oxygen can re-ignite them. A confrontation with pain from an earlier period in your life and unprocessed emotions can reappear at any moment during contact. This often happens when you experience a new loss – if, for example, you fall ill, have a burn-out or get a divorce, or if your birth parents or adoptive or foster parents become ill or pass away. But it can also happen at a beautiful, meaningful moment in your life – for example, if you get married or have (grand)children.

David (30), a former foster child, tells how difficult the confrontation with your past can be:[61]

> My father became seriously ill a few years ago. I realised then that I didn't have it in me to visit him often. I had flashback of my early childhood, when I felt a heavy sense of responsibility for him. I couldn't handle that another time. I could organise the district nurse and home care, and all the other services that he needed, but I didn't want to take care of him myself.

Rianne (39) tells about feelings of *powerlessness* and *sadness*:

> I have very little contact with my birth father. When I was eight, he murdered my mother. That's 31 years ago now. Since then, I've seen my father five times, talked with him on the phone twice and texted him twice. The moments of contact have always happened on my initiative. I thought it was important to know who my father was. I needed to see him, so that I could make progress in processing my loss. In the meantime, I've become an adult and I have two children, eight and five years old. The function of the meetings is changing now that I have children. They ask questions and they're curious. That means that my role is changing, which is something that I'm very much aware of. Still, there are always feelings of loss and sadness, which sometimes make it difficult for me to function. The fact that I hardly have any contact with my father bothers me. People think that I shouldn't want to have any contact with him, after all that he's done to me. On the one hand, I

can understand that very well, but, on the other, it also gives me a very powerless feeling. Why does it have to be that way…?

The feelings of loss in the contact with your parents can be so intense *that you choose never again to allow your father or your mother into your life.* Adolescents can also choose to keep the door closed temporarily in an act of self-defence. Joanne (42), a former foster child, tells about her contact with her birth father during puberty:

> After I had been living, out of necessity, on my own (I was 16 at the time) for several weeks, my father came to tell me that a new foster family had been found for me. He wanted to take me to them. I told him that that was out of the question and I refused to go with him. While the child in me had opened the door to him and had maintained contact with love, the teen in me slammed the door shut in his face. A man from the pedagogical office collected a bag of my things from 'home' and took me away. In my heart I had decided not to let my father in again.
>
> The feelings of horror, revulsion and, to my regret, also hatred, at times, lasted a long time. Now that I'm older I can see that they were especially emotions with which I could protect myself from him. The unwanted bond that we had cost me an awful lot of energy. In fact, I constantly lived in resistance against him and everything he stood for. But when I became an adult, something else began to occur to me, the need to forgive, to feel affection, to just be.

It was only after she turned 30 that she was able to 'leave the door ajar':

> He came to my birthday celebration once and met my mother-in-law whom I held in great esteem. The two of them had a lively conversation and she later told me that she thought I had a very charming father. At moments like that, you can make a new choice. Are you going to acknowledge the other, charming side? Are you going to say, he and I have that in common? Are you going to tell her about all of the things that he's done wrong or…?

I can remember that I thought about it and left the door ajar. Not long after that, my father was admitted to a hospital for a bypass. I went to the hospital with my brother. While my father was recovering from the anaesthetic, I realised that I was secretly stroking him. I surprised myself no end. Later on I was very upset about it. I can still see myself sitting on his bed, knowing and feeling that I still loved him. I thought that I was horrible, moved, hopeless, weak and ridiculous all at once.

Although this marked the beginning of a process of acceptance, I still continued to resist and be abrasive. There was so much anger in me about the past. I was 34 when my father died. Until that time, and also afterwards, I was still on my guard to see that there wasn't any new damage done. But as my dependence on him diminished, I was better able to see my father for what he was and what he had done and what he had not done.

Manuel (28), adopted from Columbia, experiences *anger* more than anything else in his contact with his birth parents. He always had a hard time in the adoptive family where he grew up:

I was six when I was adopted by Dutch parents. They lived in a small village and were very religious. In Colombia I'd lived on the streets for a long time and now I suddenly had to pray and eat with a knife and fork. It was a huge shock. I was never able to get used to life with my adoptive parents. As I remember it, my whole youth was taken up with commands and prohibitions. I don't remember any laughter or any hugging in our house. I left home when I was 16, and very soon after that I went in search of my birth parents. I had a powerful feeling of recognition from the moment I saw them and I cried my eyes out with joy. We've had frequent contact ever since. But at the same time, I have an ambivalent relationship with my birth parents. One the one hand, I'm happy that they're back in my life, but, on the other, the anger swells up in me when I think about what they did to me. If they'd taken better care of me, I wouldn't have had to spend those years in Friesland. That can't be undone and, however hard I try, I cannot forget about all those lost years. The anger rises up especially at times when things aren't going well in my life.

Adoptee and former foster child Josh (33) experiences *insecurity* and *disappointment* in the contact with his birth mother. He just can't manage to form a real bond with his mother:

> As a child, I lived in lots of different institutions and children's homes. I finally ended up with a very nice foster family. They helped me to get my life on track. When I was 13, we began looking for my mother. We organised a real search and eventually we found her. I was so happy! But when I met her, my joy melted like snow under the sun. She was cold and indifferent, and when we left, I had an empty feeling inside of me. For years after I've tried to break through her indifference. I've tried contacting her again and again, and every time I've been disappointed. My mother wasn't interested in me and that still hurts. I'm 33 now and I haven't visited my mother for a few years. At the moment I just don't need those chilly confrontations.

The Circle of Connecting

In order to make the feelings of loss that you experience from contact with your parents more manageable, you can make use of various themes from the Circle of Connecting:

- *The body (Theme 1)*: make sure that you eat well, drink well and get enough sleep, and that your get enough exercise and fresh air. The condition that your body is in has a large influence on how you feel. If you've had a stressful meeting, take some time the next day to get back into balance.

- *The mind (Theme 2)*: consider your automatic thoughts and beliefs and write them down. Are they realistic? What thoughts and beliefs might be (more) helpful to you? Which ones won't be? Take the time to prepare for a contact moment with your birth parent(s). Consider carefully what you should expect. If your expectations are realistic, then you're less likely to be disappointed afterwards. Take your time to think about things and simultaneously limit that time so you won't drown in thoughts and beliefs which are constantly demanding your attention.

- *The heart (Theme 3)*: make room for sadness or pain. This loss is part of your life. It won't go away. Try to stop fighting against your feelings. Make sure that you have a good breathing technique and develop your body awareness, so you won't drown in your emotions. All of your feelings are allowed to be there. The pain that you feel has to do with a shortage of love and with those things that cannot be part of your life (any more). Allow yourself to laugh or to make the most awful jokes. Humour can be liberating and sometimes healing, too.

- *The surroundings (Theme 4)*: make sure that you have enough support from your friends and/or family. With whom can you share your thoughts and feelings about the contact? Who is there who actually sees you and listens to you? Stay up late one evening, talking with friends about a meeting that you've had. Do you know of anyone who's had a similar experience and might discuss things with you? Do you need the sympathetic ear of a professional care-giver? Take the time to express yourself.

- *The past (Theme 5)*: look for the missing pieces to the puzzle and the supplementary stories in so far as you don't have these yet. They can give you the answers to important questions. Make your past more tangible with the help of life-books, picture albums or a diary. Take a course in writing; put the stories of your past down on paper. You can also write in the third person rather than the 'I' form. It's often easier to write about things then. (It allows you to take some distance from what's happened.) Talk with your family about the past. Make as many beautiful memories visible as you can, so that you won't forget them. Try to make the context of your sadness visible by getting more information, by participating in a family constellation or making a genogram.

- *The present (Theme 6)*: take conscious leave after every moment of contact. Take something that was valuable to you and leave something behind that you don't want to take with you. Think of a ritual with which you mark important connecting moments. These rituals remind you of the good moments, even if you're going through a rough patch. What connects you? How can you express that? If you feel a lot of pain about something that's happened, you can also make a ritual for that painful moment. If you give it a visible or tangible form, it often becomes easier to take some distance from it afterwards. Put reflecting questions to yourself, as in the section 'Making sense of your experience' (p.132), and try as much as possible to make sense of your relationship.

- *The future (Theme 7)*: think about your values and those of your birth parent(s). How do they differ? How are they the same? How can you give form to your shared values? Is it possible that they can be a connecting element? Accept that your parents are who they are. Stop fighting against what is. Loss will always be part of your life. Adoptee and former foster child Sharita (44) has this to say about it:

Since I've met my birth mother, I've had lots of intense emotions. On the inside, I'm just like my mother, but I have the value system of my adoptive mother. So we differ a great deal despite everything that we have in common. Being in touch with her is far from easy. Three years ago, we had a very nasty conflict. As a result, we're following a different path. Our relationship isn't travelling on a main road any more, but on a secondary road. That decision has given me some peace of mind. It's led to a measure of acceptance. But although they say that it's better not to look back, that's easier said than done in our case. I can't forget that nasty conflict that we had three years ago.

On the other hand, I've gained a lot from contact with my birth mother too. If you were to ask me whether I'd do it all over again, then I can say without hesitation that I would. There's a bump on every road. I enjoy the things that are there and learn from the ones that aren't. And my birth mother is the reason I'm here in this world after all. I have no bitterness, but sometimes I feel disappointment and a tinge of loss. That's the way life is.

Questions
Knowledge questions

1. Foster children are usually in frequent contact with one or both of their birth parents when they are young. For the child's process of mourning, it is generally important that the foster parents and the birth parents accept each other. Why is that so important?

2. Adopted children sometimes have contact with their birth parents during their youth. That can provide peace of mind and recognition, but it can also summon up strong feelings of loss. What can adopted children grieve about? Think of a few examples.

    a. Children are sometimes able to mourn their losses to a limited extent only. Why is that?

    b. How can adoptive and foster parents support their child in the process of mourning?

    c. How can you constructively deal with postponed mourning later in life?

3. If you are afraid of being rejected, then there's a chance that you'll avoid a meeting. Which steps from the Circle of Connecting can you use to prepare yourself in any case for a possible meeting?

4. A rejection says nothing about the one searching and everything about the vulnerability or the powerlessness of the birth parents. There can be many reasons for their rejection. Why is it difficult to consider those reasons after

a rejection? Which steps in the Circle of Connecting are the most important in the first instance?

5. Sometimes adoptees and former foster children feel depressed after the first meeting. That can happen, for example, because you had unrealistic expectations before the meeting. Give three examples of unrealistic thoughts that can lead to depression after a meeting. For each thought give a realistic or helpful variant.

6. After a meeting, it's important that you make sense of what has happened to you. What does it mean to 'make sense of' something? Think of a number of reflecting question that you could put to yourself after a meeting.

   a. Anger is a complicated emotion. What needs can underlie anger?

   b. Sometimes anger is very functional. It can help you to protect yourself. Think of an example where anger works in this way.

Personal questions

1. What feelings of loss do you experience in your continuing contact with your birth parents? How have you dealt with those feelings of loss so far? Think of three other ways of dealing with them.

2. Are there steps in the Circle of Connecting that you would like to take in order to progress further in the process of mourning? Which steps are they? How could you give them concrete form now?

Appendix
Values[62]

What values do you think are most important in your life? Underline them. You can add other values to the list if you like. Which fit you best? Choose at least ten. Which four or five values do you think are most important?

1. Accepting: embracing life as it comes; being open and accepting of yourself, others, life, etc.

2. Being present: being in touch with yourself and your surroundings; concentrating fully on what you are busy with and on those who are with you.

3. Assertiveness: speaking up for yourself with peace of mind and self-confidence; having the courage to advocate the things you believe in; knowing your own values and defending yourself without feelings of guilt; treating yourself with respect.

4. Thoughtfulness: giving careful attention to the needs of others and making decisions in a thoughtful way; taking into consideration the feelings of others.

5. Authenticity: being real, faithful to your own values and convictions.

6. Modesty: being modest or humble; letting your achievements speak for themselves.

7. Reliability: living up to the trust that others have in you; being someone who others can rely on.

8. Contributing: making a positive contribution to something.

9. Creativity: being open to inspiration and originality; being resourceful and intuitive.

10. Gratitude: living with a constant attitude of appreciation and gratitude for life as it is unfolding.

11. Stamina: being determined to finish what you've started, despite the obstacles that you encounter on your way.

12. Honesty: being honest, truthful and sincere with yourself and with others.

13. Flexibility: being able to adapt to the changing conditions of life, with resilience and confidence; bending with the flow and recognising the challenge in that.

14. Patience: having the quiet hope that everything will work out; trusting the cycle of life, without urgency.

15. Equality: treating others as your equals and vice versa.

16. Generosity: being generous and liberal towards yourself and others; sharing what you have; sharing what you have with others; giving to someone else something that is valuable to you.

17. Hope: looking to the future with trust and faith; keeping the faith to try again.

18. Empathy: being empathetic about the feelings and thoughts of others, with the result that you understand others better.

19. Integrity: honouring agreements; being reliable for others; doing what you say you'll do and defending what you think is right.

20. Intimacy: being open and vulnerable emotionally or physically in close relationships.

21. Intuition: having access to the wisdom of your intuition in order to gain insight, to discover the truth; reflecting in silence, being open to clarity, trusting that an answer will come at the right moment; allowing yourself to be led by the universe.

22. Strength: living according to your inner capacity to handle everything that comes your way.

23. Compliance: being patient and accepting in difficult circumstances; dealing with problems with confidence.

24. Love: having deep affection for yourself and others and treating them with tenderness.

25. Loyalty: having unwavering commitment to people and ideals that are important to you.

26. Moderation: being satisfied with enough; knowing your own perfect rhythm which enables you to choose precisely enough.

27. Compassion: feeling deep compassion for yourself or another, without being judgemental.

28. Kindness: giving tender attention to yourself and others; taking yourself and others into consideration.

29. Courage: doing what has to be done, with resoluteness and without hesitation, when confronted with fear, a threat or difficulties; being brave.

30. Curiosity: being open and interested; investigating things and making discoveries.

31. Sacrifice: being prepared to give up something important for something even more important; giving up everything for a worthy cause.

32. Independence: being autonomous; standing on your own two feet and doing things your own way; respecting at the same time the values and boundaries of others.

33. Entrepreneurial spirit: being original and creative in what you do; boldly giving expression to new ideas; having an eye for new possibilities and ideas and carrying them out.

34. Openness: sharing your thoughts and ideas without a hidden agenda; looking at things from the perspective of others and weighing all of the arguments against each other without bias.

35. Cheerfulness: seeing the lighter side of the things; maintaining a positive attitude of optimism and confidence.

36. Sincerity: being open and genuine; your words and your deeds reflecting a heart full of truth, your deeds inspired by pure intentions.

37. Stability: being true to your goal, whatever happens; not allowing yourself to be turned from your course; like a strong ship in a storm, sailing on the tops of the waves.

38. Justice: wanting to solve problems honestly and without deceit; seeking the truth without speaking badly about others or being judgemental.

39. Respect: being considerate toward yourself, others and towards the earth and all living creatures.

40. Cooperation: working together with others, putting your shoulders into something; standing next to each other and using the talents that each one has to offer.

41. Beauty: admiring and observing the harmony, colour and loveliness of the world; living in beauty.

42. Tact: weighing your words; reflecting before you speak your mind – for example, when you're angry.

43. Dedication: working with inner passion, with enthusiasm and animation; striving with all of your heart for what you believe in and care about.

44. Resoluteness: directing your energy at your goal and not wavering until your goal has been reached; using your willpower to act with focus.

45. Resilience: discovering the hope and spiritual strength to recover during times of adversity.

46. Responsibility: being responsible for your words and actions and answerable for what you do.

47. Forgiveness: letting mistakes go and releasing bitterness; releasing pain to allow for the possibility for a new beginning.

48. Wonder: being open to the beauty and mystery of life.

49. Reciprocity: building up relationships in which there is a fair balance between giving and taking.

50. Certainty: moving forward resolutely according to your sense of truth; not shifting with the mood of the moment, knowing that this is the way you want to go.

51. Self-control: using your discipline in order to do what you have chosen to do; not allowing yourself to be tossed back and forth by the winds of your desire.

52. Self-development: continuing to grow, advance or improve in knowledge, skills, character or experience of life; continuing to challenge yourself to grow and learn.

53. Caring: giving gentle attention to people and things which are important to you.

54. Wisdom: being able to distinguish the correct path at the right moment; living with maturity and patience to make decisions which can be accepted; living beyond your thoughts to a deeper knowledge.

Bibliography

Brodzinsky, D., Schlechter, M.D. and Henig, R.M. (2003) *Being Adopted: The Lifelong Search for Self*. New York, NY: Doubleday.

Broos, R. and Vankeirsbulck, X. (2012) *Mijn ouders zijn mijn ouders niet* [*My Parents Aren't My Real Parents*]. Leuven: Sajam.be.

van Dongen, M. (2013) *De Adoptiemonologen* [*The Adoption Monologues*]. Schiedam: Scriptum Psychologie.

Dudevsky, S. (2013) *Valse start, de gevolgen van een verstoorde jeugd* [*False Start: Consequences of a Disturbed Youth. Interviews with Adult Former Foster Children*]. Rotterdam: Lemniscaat.

Feast, J., Seabrook, S. and Webb, E. (2002) *Preparing for Reunion: Experiences from the Adoption Circle*. London: The Children's Society.

Harris, R. (2009) *ACT Made Simple: An Easy-to-Read Primer on Acceptance and Commitment Therapy*. Oakland, CA: New Harbinger Publications.

Harris, R. (2011) *The Confidence Gap: From Fear to Freedom*. Boston, MA: Shambhala Publications.

Harris, R. (2012) *The Reality Slap: Finding Peace and Fulfilment When Life Hurts*. Oakland, CA: New Harbinger Publications.

Hoksbergen, R. (2006) *Vertraagde start, geadopteerden aan het woord* [*Delayed Beginning: Interviews with Adult Adoptees*]. Soest: Aspekt.

de Jong, T. (2011) *In huis en hart. Interviews met pleegouders* [*In My House and in My Heart: Interviews with Foster Parents*]. Assen: Van Gorcum/Mobiel.

Lifton, B.J. (2009) *Lost and Found: The Adoption Experience*. Ann Arbor, MI: University of Michigan Press.

Maes, J. (2007) *Leven met gemis, handboek over rouw, rouwbegeleiding en rouwtherapie* [*Living with Loss: Handbook of Grief, Grief Counselling and Grief Therapy*]. Baarn: Agora.

Mittendorf, C. and Muller, E. (1998) *Ik ben er kapot van, over psychotrauma en de verwerking van schokkende gebeurtenissen* [*I am Dreadfully Cut-up by it: Psychotrauma and the Processing of Shocking Events*]. Amsterdam: Boom Uitgevers.

de Mönnink, H.J. (2008) *Verlieskunde, handreiking voor de beroepspraktijk* [*The Science of Loss and Grief*]. Amsterdam/Doetinchem: Reed Business.

Noten, S. (2010) *Stapeltjesverdriet, stilstaan bij wat is [Piled Grief: Research on the Influence of Loss in Very Young Children (0–4 years)]*. Heeze: In de Wolken.

Servan-Schreiber, D. (2005) *The Instinct to Heal: Curing Depression, Anxiety and Stress Without Drugs and Without Talk Therapy*. Emmaus, PA: Rodale Press.

Stroebe, M.S and Schut, H. (1999) 'The dual process model of coping with bereavement: rationale and description.' *Death Studies 23*, 197–224.

Tieman, W., van der Ende, J. and Verhulst, F. (2008) 'Young adult international adoptees' search for birth parents.' *Journal of Family Psychology 22*, 5.

Trinder, E., Feast, J. and Howe, D. (2005) *The Adoption Reunion Handbook*. Chichester: John Wiley and Sons.

Verrier, N. (2003) *The Primal Wound: Understanding the Adopted Child*. Louisville, KY: Gateway Press.

van Well, C. (2012) *Geadopteerd, en dan? Persoonlijke verhalen van geadopteerden, afstandsmoeders en adoptieouders [Adopted, and Then? Personal Stories of Adult Adoptees, Birth Mothers and Adoptive Parents]*. Utrecht: De Graaff.

Welscher, M. (2012) *Adoptiepubers, gesprekken met pubers en ouders [Adopted Teens: Interviews with Teenagers and Parents]*. Wijk en Aalburg: Den Brug.

Wolfs, R. (2008) *Adoption Conversations: What, When and How to Tell*. London: BAAF.

Wolfs, R. (2010) *More Adoption Conversations: What, When and How to Tell*. London: BAAF.

William Worden, J. (2001) *Grief Counseling and Grief Therapy: A Handbook for the Mental Health Practitioner*. New York, NY: Springer Publishing Company.

Further Reading

ADOPTION

Brodzinsky, D.M. (1992) *Being Adopted: The Lifelong Search for Self*. New York, NY: Doubleday.

Cornbluth, Sue (2014), *Building Self-Esteem in Children and Teens Who Are Adopted or Fostered*. London: Jessica Kingsley Publishers.

Eldridge, Sherrie (2015) *Twenty Life Transforming Choices Adoptees Need to Make*. London: Jessica Kingsley Publishers.

Harris, Perlita (2012) *Chosen: Living with adoption*. London: British Association for Adoption and Fostering.

Lifton, Betty Jean (1995) *Journey Of The Adopted Self: A Search for Wholeness*. New York, NY: Basic Books.

Lifton, Betty Jean (2009) *Lost and Found: The Adoption Experience*. Ann Arbor, MI: The University of Michigan Press.

Verrier, N. (1993) *The Primal Wound: Understanding the Adopted Child*. Baltimore, MD: Gateway Press.

Xinran (2010) *Message from an Unknown Chinese Mother: Stories of the Lost Daughters of China*. London: Chatto and Windus.

TRAUMA AND LOSS

Kolk, Bessel van der (2014) *The Body Keeps the Score: Mind, Brain and Body in the Transformation of Trauma*. London: Allen Lane.

Levine, Peter (2006), *Trauma Through a Child's Eyes: Awakening the Ordinary Miracle of Healing*. Berkeley, CA: North Atlantic Books.

Levine, Peter (2008), *Healing Trauma: A Pioneering Program for Restoring the Wisdom of Your Body*. Louisville, CA: Sounds True.

Levine, Peter (1997) *Waking the Tiger: Healing Trauma – The Innate Capacity to Transform Overwhelming Experiences*. Berkeley, CA: North Atlantic Books.

Levine, P.A. (2012) *Freedom from Pain: Discover Your Body's Power to Overcome Physical Pain*. Louisville, CA: Sounds True.

Rothschild, Babette (2010) *8 Keys to Safe Trauma Recovery: Take-charge Strategies to Empower Your Healing* (8 Keys to Mental Health). New York, NY: W. W. Norton & Company.

Viorst, J. (1998) *Necessary Losses: The Loves, Illusions, Dependencies, and Impossible Expectations that All of Us Have to Give Up in Order to Grow*. New York, NY: Fireside.

Wimberger, Lisa (2015) *Neurosculpting: A Whole-Brain Approach to Heal Trauma, Rewrite Limiting Beliefs, and Find Wholeness*. Louisville, CA: Sounds True.

COPING AND NON-COPING THOUGHTS/RATIONAL EMOTIVE BEHAVIOR THERAPY (REBT)

Ellis, Albert (2001) *Overcoming Destructive Beliefs, Feelings, and Behaviors*. Amhearst, NY: Prometheus Books.

Ellis, Albert (1999) *How to Make Yourself Happy and Remarkably Less Disturbable*. Atascadero, CA: Impact Publishers.

Garcy, Pamela D. (2009), *The REBT Super-Activity Guide: 52 Weeks of REBT For Clients, Groups, Students, and YOU!* CreateSpace Independent Publishing Platform.

WRITING AND AUTOBIOGRAPHIC WRITING

Ledoux, Denis (2006) *Turning Memories Into Memoirs: A Handbook for Writing Lifestories*. Lisbon Falls, ME: Soleil Press.

Ledoux, Denis (1998) *The Photo Scribe: A Writing Guide/How to Write the Stories Behind Your Photographs*. Lisbon Falls, ME: Soleil Press.

MINDFULNESS

Bohlmeijer, E. (2013) *A Beginner's Guide to Mindfulness: Live in the Moment*. Maidenhead: Open University Press.

Maex, E. (2014) *Mindfulness: In the Maelstrom of Life*. Tielt, Belgium: Lannoo Publishers.

Stahl, B. and Goldstein, E. (2010) *A Mindfulness-Based Stress Reduction Workbook*. Oakland, CA: New Harbinger Publications.

Van Vreeswijk, M., Broersen, J. and Schurink, G. (2014) *Mindfulness and Schema Therapy: A Practical Guide*. Chichester, UK: Wiley Blackwell.

Williams, Mark (2011) *Mindfulness: A practical guide to finding peace in a frantic world*. London: Piatkus.

BREATHING

Farh, Donna (1996) *The Breathing Book: Vitality and Good Health Through Essential Breath Work*. New York, NY: Henry Holt and Company.

Manné, Joy (2013) *Conscious Breathing in Everyday Life: Know Your Breath: Know Yourself*. CreateSpace Independent Publishing Platform.

HEART COHERENCE/HEALTH: STRESS REDUCTION

Childre, Doc and Martin, Howard (2000) *The HeartMath Solution: The Institute of HeartMath's Revolutionary Program for Engaging the Power of the Heart's Intelligence.* San Francisco, CA: HarperOne.

Childre, Doc and Rozman, Deborah, Ph.D (2003) *Transforming Anger: The HeartMath Solution for Letting Go of Rage, Frustration, and Irritation.* Oakland, CA: New Harbinger.

Childre, Doc and Rozman, Deborah, Ph.D (2005) *Transforming Stress: The HeartMath Solution for Relieving Worry, Fatigue, and Tension.* Oakland, CA: New Harbinger.

Childre, Doc and Rozman, Deborah, Ph.D (2006) *Transforming Anxiety: The HeartMath Solution for Overcoming Fear and Worry and Creating Serenity.* Oakland, CA: New Harbinger.

Childre, Doc and Rozman, Deborah, Ph.D (2007), *Transforming Depression: The HeartMath Solution to Feeling Overwhelmed, Sad, and Stressed.* Oakland, CA: New Harbinger. HeartMath, available at www.hearthmath.com. (On this website readers can find much information and products that can help you with inner balance and heart coherence.)

Servan-Schreiber, D. (2004) *The Instinct to Heal: Curing Depression, Anxiety and Stress Without Drugs and Without Talk Therapy.* Emmaus, PA: Rodale Press.

Wimburger, Lisa (2012) *New Beliefs, New Brain: Free Yourself From Stress And Fear.* Richmond, CA: Divine Arts.

ACCEPTANCE AND COMMITMENT THEORY (ACT)

Harris, R. (2008) *The Happiness Trap: How to Stop Struggling and Start Living: A Guide to ACT.* Boston, MA: Trumpeter.

Harris, R. (2012) *The Reality Slap: Finding Peace and Fulfilment When Life Hurts.* Oakland, CA: New Harbinger Publications.

Hayes, S.C. (2005) *Get Out of Your Mind and Into Your Life: The New Acceptance and Commitment Therapy.* Oakland, CA: New Harbinger Publications.

SYSTEMIC WORK: FAMILY CONSTELLATIONS

Manné, J. and Hellinger, B. (2009) *Family Constellations: A Practical Guide to Uncovering the Origins of Family Conflict.* Berkeley, CA: North Atlantic Books.

Torsten Preiss, Indra (2012) *Family Constellations Revealed: Hellinger's Family and other Constellations Revealed (The Systemic View Book 1).* CreateSpace Independent Publishing Platform.

Endnotes

Chapter 1

1. This classification is based on de Mönnick 2008, p.37.
2. 'Tasks of mourning' is a notion first introduced by William Worden (2001).
3. In Stroebe and Schut 1999, the terms 'loss-orientated' and 'restoration-orientated' are introduced for the first time. According to de Mönnick (2008), the term 'restoration-orientated' is in fact a metaphor which implies that you 'return to the former state'. For that reason, I am using the term 'constructive-orientated'; this is a metaphor which is directed to the process of transformation into something new.
4. From 'Rouwen doe je niet van fase 1, naar 2, tot en met 4' ['Mourning isn't something one does from phase 1 to phase 2 till phase 5'], NRC weekend, 26 October 2013.
5. I have been inspired here by the eight mourning challenges of Johan Maes (2007, p.87–98).
6. Mittendorf and Muller 1998.
7. The classification is based on de Mönnick 2008: impact, coping and support.
8. Hoksbergen 2006, p.209.

Chapter 2

9. Van Dongen 2013, p.98.
10. De Jong 2011, p.136.
11. Hoksbergen 2006, p.207.
12. Van Well 2012, p.122.
13. Hoksbergen 2006, p.228.
14. Van Dongen 2013, p.126.
15. Hoksbergen 2006, .p.120.
16. Van Dongen, p.151.
17. Hoksbergen 2006, p.147
18. Van Dongen, p.171.

19. Interview with van Dongen, *Volkskrant*.
20. Van Dongen, p.107.
21. Hoksbergen 2006, p.32.
22. Broos and Vankeirsbulck 2012, p.109.
23. Van Dongen, p.35.
24. Hoksbergen 2006, p.50.
25. Broos and Vankeirsbulck 2012, p.27.
26. Hoksbergen 2006, p.202.
27. Hoksbergen 2006, pp.338–339.
28. De Jong, p.170.
29. Hoksbergen 2006, p. 223

Chapter 3

30. Hoksbergen 2006, p.342
31. Servan-Schreiber 2005, p.176, footnote 11 in Dutch edition
32. Servan-Schreiber 2005, p.145 in Dutch edition.
33. Hoksbergen 2006, p.205.
34. Hoksbergen 2006, p.54.
35. Van Well 2012, p.126.
36. Hoksbergen 2006, p.50.
37. Van Dongen, p.153.
38. Van Dongen, p.193.
39. Van Well 2012, p.53.
40. *Worldchildren Magazine 1*, 2013.
41. Broos and Vankeirsbulck 2012, p.104.
42. Van Well 2012, p.133.
43. 'Geen bepaald actieplan' ['Not a certain plan of action'], interview with Anneke Vinke. Available at http://blogadoptie.wordpress.com/2014/01/14/interview-geen-bepaald-actieplan (accessed 9 January 2015).
44. Tieman, van der Ende, and Verhulst 2008.
45. Popular television programme in the Netherlands in which adults search for biological family members.
46. Van Well 2012, pp.93–94.
47. Blog 'Speciaal voor volwassenen die geadopteerd zijn' ['Especially for adults who are adopted'], 25 September 2012.
48. Hoksbergen 2006, p.265.
49. Harris 2009, p.25.
50. Van Dongen, pp.195–196.

Chapter 4

51. Welscher 2012, pp.21–22.
52. De Jong, p.67.
53. Broos and Vankeirsbulck 2012, p.114.

54. Wolfs 2008, p.50.
55. *Spoorloos*, 18 February 2013.
56. Broos and Vankeirsbulck 2012, p.115.
57. Welscher 2012, pp.21–22.
58. *Spoorloos*, 9 September 2013.
59. Based in part on Trinder, Feast and Howe 2005.
60. Trinder, Feast and Howe 2005, p.109.
61. De Jong 2011, p.170.

Appendix

62. In creating this list I was particularly inspired by the list of values in Russ Harris in *The Confidence Gap* (2011) and *The Reality Slap* (2012); some of the values are re-translations from the Dutch translation of *The Reality Slap*.

Index